Aseem Juneja is an entrepreneur and a prominent voice in the Indian stock market regulatory space with almost two decades of experience.

He is the founder of A Digital Blogger, a YouTube channel dedicated to stock market insights, and *Stock Pathshala*, an education platform for traders and investors. Aseem has been instrumental in helping retail traders navigate the complexities of the market.

His work focuses on exposing misleading narratives and protecting investors from fraudulent schemes. He has spent nearly a decade educating retail traders about the hidden risks, manipulations and scams lurking in the financial ecosystem.

When not working, he enjoys spending time with his kids while continuing to pursue his entrepreneurial ambitions.

FRAUD FREE

HOW TO OUTSMART SCAMMERS
AND KEEP YOUR MONEY SAFE

ASEEM JUNEJA

RUPA

Published by
Rupa Publications India Pvt. Ltd 2025
161-B/4, Gulmohar House,
Yusuf Sarai Community Centre,
New Delhi 110049

Sales centres:
Bengaluru Chennai
Hyderabad Kolkata Mumbai

P-ISBN: 978-93-7003-208-8
E-ISBN: 978-93-7003-591-1

First impression 2025

10 9 8 7 6 5 4 3 2 1

Printed in India

CONTENTS

Part 5: Stock-Market Education Scams

Part 6: SEBI's Fine Line

ABBREVIATIONS

BSE	Bombay Stock Exchange
CIS	Collective investment scheme
IA	Investment advisor
IPO	Initial public offering
KYC	Know your customer
NIDA	National Institute of Drug Abuse in India
NSE	National Stock Exchange
OG finfluencers	Original financial influencers
PFUTP	Prohibition of Fraudulent and Unfair Trading Practices
PMO	Prime Minister's Office
PMS	Portfolio management services
PRAHAR	Public Response against Helplessness & Action for Redressal
PRS	Premium research service
RA	Research analyst
SCORES	SEBI Complaints Redress System
SEBI	Securities and Exchange Board of India
SMART ODR	Securities Market Approach for Resolution through Online Dispute Resolution
SMEs	Subject-matter experts

INTRODUCTION

The number of retail traders in India has seen a mammoth jump in the last five years, from 10,795,660 to 50,214,191 active demat accounts.[1] While Covid did have a part to play, it's been some time now and the Covid effect has dimmed in the subsequent years. However, the growth in the number of traders has not paused. This means they are here to stay. But along with this rise, the number of scams in the stock market has also increased. The *kinds* of scams have jumped too.

To put this in perspective, as per the Indian Cyber Crime Coordination Centre (I4C), in the last four years Indians have lost ₹33,165 crore to stock market and cyber scams. Out of these, ₹22,812 worth of scams happened in 2024 alone. A separate study conducted by non-profit PRAHAR (Public Response against Helplessness & Action for Redressal) said, 'incidents of cyberattacks in India may reach 17 trillion by 2047.'[2] The Telangana IT & Electronics department states that Indians lose ₹1.5 lakh to cyber criminals every minute.[3]

A combination of social media influence and tech vulnerabilities has made it almost impossible to trust what one

---

[1]'Arbitration Status', NSE India, https://tinyurl.com/258pxt59. Accessed on 3 March 2025.

[2]*The Hindu* Bureau, 'Incidents of cyberattacks on India may reach 17 trillion by 2047: Study', *The Hindu*, 30 October 2014, https://tinyurl.com/2zz5j4je. Accessed on 3 March 2025.

[3]Ibid.

is watching and listening to. Even with different mechanisms and regulations in place, all sorts of scams and frauds are trapping gullible people. This was why I decided to write this book to fill a void of awareness.

People need to know what is out there. At any given moment, they could be shown, told, messaged or emailed lies they might believe to be 100 per cent true. These are ploys to expose their vulnerabilities, loot them of their savings and leave them in a situation they regret for years to come.

Fraud Free is just a small step to stop this from happening, at least for the people this book reaches.

This book is based on nine years of my experience in the securities market as a researcher, observer and content creator. It talks about the types of financial scams, how they are carried out, the lures behind them, the techniques scammers use to play with the psychology and emotions of the victim, and so much more.

Fraud Free focuses on observations and insights I have obtained through comprehensive primary research. I have tried to understand the psychology and mindset of the victim before, during and after being involved in a financial scam. In addition to talking to traders, finfluencers and victims, my team and I have even acted as clients to investigate these scams by buying and paying for courses, classes and premium Telegram subscriptions. All this gave us direct access to the modus operandi of fraudsters and the scale of their frauds. We've also talked about these scams on our YouTube channel, A Digital Blogger.

This book also shines a light on how you can actually stay away from getting duped. It will make you aware about potential scams and can quite literally keep you Fraud Free, assuming you learn something and then apply those learnings.

Part 1

OUR VERY OWN, THE STOCK MARKET!

1

STOCK MARKET AND FRAUDS

Take a deep breath and read this:

> Dear Sir,
>
> I have been scammed out of ₹2.5 lakh, all of my savings. I was told they would help me invest in an IPO privately. They gave me an app and I could see that my capital appreciated to ₹10 lakh within 20 days.
>
> I tried to withdraw a small amount but I couldn't. Now I am unable to even withdraw my capital of ₹2.5 lakh.
>
> What should I do?

This is one of the many stock-market fraud emails I read as soon as I open my inbox any given morning. Such emails and direct Instagram messages have become part of my normal routine in the last few years. Someone, somewhere was looted. Does that mean the stock market is a place of fallacy? Is it all a trap? Is scamming someone the only way people make money in the stock market?

No, absolutely not.

Let me ask you something. Why do house thefts happen? How does a highly secure bank get looted in the middle of the day? Why do people lose money in a real-estate project which is supposed to provide huge returns? The basic answers to these questions are that people let down their guard when they get careless or greedy.

And whom do they drop their guards for? People who are already waiting to pounce on them and take advantage at the right time. When it comes to the stock market, these people know how to manipulate and how to mislead beginner traders and investors.

In the past, and to an extent even today, there were many Indore/Ahmedabad/Mumbai-based advisory companies who promised an unrealistic world of daily returns. These companies ended up giving shady stock exchange tips for truckloads of money. There are brokers who have had a history of cheating their clients in the name of brokerage generation and unauthorized trading. Today, with even a slightly noticeable social media following, one can easily deceive a newbie and they won't even know they have been wronged. Some blame the victim for being scammed and that may be partially true.

There is no doubt that scamsters take advantage of gullible people but even highly-educated, experienced stock market traders and investors get looted all the time.

Here's an example of a very close friend, Varun. A couple of years back, Varun wanted to invest in real estate and knew someone in his town who had recently invested in a residential apartment. There was a rumour that this project could give five times the return in a few years. He went to the builder along with his acquaintance and the deal was done. He paid ₹60 lakh upfront to the builder. Last year, he got possession of the house.

When we met recently, he told me, 'Aseem, I am stuck, man. I bought this house for ₹1.5 crore for investment purposes but today most of the tenants are not sticking around.'

'Why? Your house is beautiful. I attended the house-warming ceremony,' I said, surprised.

'It only *looks* good. The building material is mediocre. Something is constantly breaking and the paint on the walls is wearing off. Two days back the wardrobe door just fell down. Thank God, no one was around,' he said, with a level of frustration I had never seen in him.

When I asked Varun if he had analysed or run a background check on the builder, he replied in the negative. He said, 'There was a lot of marketing being done about this project and when I went there, it seemed very genuine. I don't know what to do now.' Varun's experience with real estate seemed very similar to the emails I get regularly. I wondered if all these were somehow connected?

Here's another example. We run a stock market education app on Google Play and iOS named Stock Pathshala. This is a one-of-a-kind app where stock market tutors come with a SEBI (Securities and Exchange Board of India) background, are registered research analysts, are investment advisors, and are also NISM-certified (National Institute of Securities Market). All these tutors need to go through their PNL (profit and loss) verification. Each tutor must be profitable in the preceding three years in the stream they are going to teach in. A lot of work is done to validate the tutors who come from different parts of the country speaking different languages and trading in different formats of the stock market.

The app is a 'no assurance, no frill' solution that caters to serious stock market learners. Stock Pathshala offers live classes through webinars (60 to 75 minutes long), batches and one-on-one mentorships (across different formats of trading and investing including swing, intraday, scalping, options, positional trading and long-term investing).

When people install Stock Pathshala, our team calls them to assist with their learning programme. A decent chunk of these users genuinely wants to learn different types of trading. But there is another audience within these users. When asked what they want to learn, they ask for tips. Our team's general response is, 'We don't offer tips. Why don't you learn the concepts? It will take you 6 months to 1 year to know how to pick stocks/securities. Post that, you can continue with your setup.'

People then say no and stop answering our follow-up calls. Sometimes they even block us. When we ask why they are not interested in learning, the answers we get are strange and sometimes funny. I have put them into six brackets:

1. I can't wait for 6 months. That's a lot of time.
2. I will pay you ₹5,000 per month and then you can give me daily tips. I want to do options only.
3. I don't have time; I have a structured life.
4. I can easily learn on YouTube. Why pay?
5. I already took a course and paid ₹25,000. Courses are all a scam.
6. I follow a YouTube channel. He shares Zero Hero Tips with me. I will be rich soon anyway. I'm not interested.

There is certainly the possibility that these users might have installed Stock Pathshala thinking it was something else. As sometimes expectations don't match reality, they get disappointed. But if we do a quick post-mortem of all these answers, we can understand why stock market frauds happen.

Why Do Stock Market Frauds Happen?

People are NOT ready to wait.

It is assumed that the stock market is a place where you can get rich overnight. Now who thinks like that? Someone who doesn't really know how the stock market works. Or maybe someone who does have a basic idea but is unrealistic or irrational. Or it could be someone who is just plain greedy.

There is a possibility that such people have been wrongly influenced by the riches of people around them or on social media. Maybe they have been shown dreams and these gullible people have believed in these 'dreams' with 100 per cent conviction. There is a belief that *this is the reality and it is very much possible.*

But is it really?

If you have studied all your life to become a doctor, an engineer, a government employee, a chartered accountant, a businessman, a writer, or whatever else you are doing, you know one basic thing—it either takes theoretical and practical learning of the art or skill to do well in it.

Now, imagine if you committed to giving two hours a day for the next 200 days to consistently learning the different concepts of the stock market. That's 400 hours of rigorous practice. Shouldn't that be enough for you to get in the groove and eventually make money?

Isn't that what you really wanted?

But everyone wants money NOW. And from a place you have no idea of, to boot. So what do people end up doing? Pay someone assuming that they are going to move around magical money and say, 'Voila! Here are your ₹50 lakh, doubled.' That's not going to happen but something else will, and those are the seeds being sown right now.

Traders are ready to pay for tips.

Asking for tips from an unregistered SEBI entity is asking for a kick in the back. But people keep doing it. It's like the dopamine effect drugs give to your body. These are some of the questions people ask openly on the internet:

- Tell me which option contract shall I trade in? Shall I buy a put or a call?
- When shall I sell it? Shall I do a partial exit or not?

One wonders how people can just trust anyone. And if there's a social media footprint, people will message you, call you and request you to provide tips even if you are not SEBI-registered. A huge chunk of beginners don't even know there is a regulator named SEBI and that one needs to have a research analyst or an investment advisor (full-time or part-time) licence to offer any kind of recommendations.

There was one such case we forwarded to SEBI. We made a video about that scammer.[1] The context was about how that person was misleading their audience with an unregistered advisory. The name of the influencer was Saurabh Maurya, also known as IITian trader. People would pay him for a stock-market trading course. While he took a few minutes of private classes, eventually the session would become a live trading session where open stock-market trading calls for option contracts were shared.

Those who had paid and were part of these private sessions placed the trades based on the entry and exit prices mentioned in the influencer's live sessions.

We got an amazing response to this video in terms of general awareness. However, there were a few comments such as:

Who are you to call him out?
We follow him and he helps us a lot in trading. So what if there is no licence?
Are you jealous if he is making money?

---

[1]A Digital Blogger, 'IITian Trader is Violating SEBI Regulations on Tips, Advisory & Front Running | Fake Finfluencers 05', *YouTube*, 25 November 2023, https://tinyurl.com/54wen8nf. Accessed on 3 March 2025.

Rationality gets eaten up by blind faith. Once you become a *fan* of someone, your mindset cannot accept any of the person's fallacies. You will defend their wrongs too. This gives confidence to such swindlers to keep doing what they have been doing. So yes, if people can take loans and steal money to pay for drugs, paying for tips isn't that different. More on this in Chapter 2.

People don't have time for learning.

Why does someone really trade? To make money.

Saying you don't have time to learn trading is not unreasonable. There is a huge possibility that with studies, a job, household chores, or a business, you might not really have much time left to learn anything new.

In that case, what can you do?

Either you don't trade or if you really want to, then you must use the services of a professional investment advisor, as anyone will tell you. However, nobody knows these providers since a major chunk of registered advisors do not have a social media presence.

Let me tell you about some of my friends.

They are software engineers, entrepreneurs, real-estate builders, government jobbers, freelancers, homemakers—the list goes on. All of them want to trade in the stock market. If one of them tell me they want to join a Telegram channel because there are tips and profit screenshots being shared, I first make fun of them and then I give them the following advice.

> *Don't hand your hard-earned money over to a social media star who does not even know what they are doing with all the influence they have. It's just mis-influence.*

I tell them to look for SEBI-registered investment advisors (IA). There are over 950 of them and this is how you can find them:

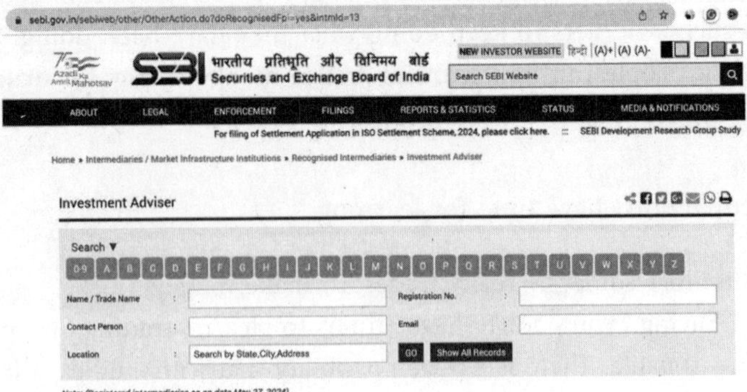

You may even look for research analysts (RA) and pick one out of the 1,200-plus that the regulator has licensed. It's easy to find them here:

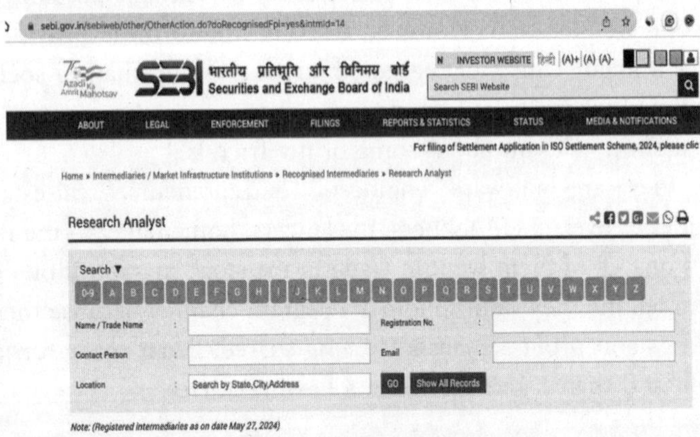

While IAs will give you personalized advice on investments, RAs provide their clients with market tips for trading and investing on a regular basis.

Even when getting assistance from these regulated advisors, you still need to validate what you are being recommended and not just follow blindly. Having said that, if you still decide to go for any of the self-proclaimed 'stock market gurus' out there, it's just telling fraudsters that you are gullible.

I can easily learn from YouTube. Why pay?

Of course you can learn from YouTube. When you begin, you must always start from there. YouTube has single-handedly revolutionized the concept of teaching and learning across the spectrum of different fields. I mean forget trading, you can learn astronomy, filmmaking, painting, cooking, professional photography, different fields of science, dancing, exercising, and everything else under the sun. Learning from YouTube from a reliable channel is not a bad idea. You just have to be consistent while forming a habit of learning. A lot of serious traders and investors follow that advice.

But what do you think a major chunk of people really do?

Since they can't wait for six months, they get swayed by the lies or misrepresentations shown on these social media sites. When that happens, the learning path on that very platform gets blurred. Free learning content where the stock market is being taught seriously now seems like full of boredom.

Paying for something makes you value it. Plus, if you are learning from somewhere reliable, there will be a structured teaching methodology. This is in line with our school education where we move from one class to another, after spending a whole year in each. This proves a commitment to learning. The same concept on a much smaller scale needs to be applied here. That's it.

Already took a course and paid ₹25,000. It's all a scam.

There is a saying in Hindi, '*Dudh ka jala chhachh bhi phoonk phoonk kar pita hai.*' This essentially translates to: if something wrong has happened to you, you will always be much more careful if you try to attempt the same thing again. People become biased against or scared of trying the same thing again. The same concept applies in the world of stock market.

Let me walk you through a personal incident.

When I was a kid, I was on my way to my town with my family. We were all coming back from a wedding. I put my hand out of the van we were in. Suddenly something happened and I saw the driver jerk the steering wheel quickly. The Maruti van flipped to its right side. It was still moving with all its four tyres facing the left side of the road. My hand that was out the window was injured really badly.

It took me a month-long hospital stay and four surgeries for the doctors to save my hand. It's been 35 years since then and I have never put my hand out of any vehicle since then. Thus, once something bad happens to you, the fear associated with that stays with you for life.

Similarly, if you have been scammed once, everything feels like a scam. Therefore, the response that someone has already taken a course and lost ₹25,000 or ₹2.5 lakh is completely valid. But why did you choose to pay such hefty amounts? I know people have paid up to ₹10 lakh for shady courses.

Before you buy a course from anyone, you need to ask yourself some questions:

- What is being told to you to sell such a course? Is it realistic or do YOU just want it to be real?
- Are you being told things like: 'Don't worry, we will make you a trader, we can make anyone a trader!' 'All

our traders are profitable.' 'We have a unique strategy that never fails.' Anything that is superlative in its form or claims to be perfect is a strong signal that it is 100 per cent not true.

- Are you being told that you will be made to trade live with the instructor? If the answer is YES, that implies the focus is on a painkiller that has a temporary impact, versus a vitamin tablet that if given consistently can change you positively forever.

I follow a YouTube channel. It shares Zero Hero tips with me. I'm not interested in learning.

Can you learn swimming just by watching YouTube videos? Or learn how to play cricket? Oh, why don't you climb a mountain the next time you watch a video about it?

Doesn't sound possible, does it?

YouTube videos can teach you to an extent. You can be taught mediocre information if you start watching any video and start doing what is being mentioned. If someone is following fancy zero-to-hero tips, there is hardly anything that can be done. The person has become an addict. Till they see what loss of financial health is, it is almost impossible to make them realize where this will eventually end up. Unfortunately, this happens a lot and there is no cure to this.

The strange part about such people is not that they won't listen because they are a fan of someone. It is that psychologically this person is looking for a magic dose. This can come from forex trading, options, binary trading, or even—and I am not kidding—from making a team on a sports betting app.

A report by Axis Mutual Fund Asset Management deduced that Indian traders, especially from tier 3 towns with an average

age of 29 years to 35 years, have gamified the concept of options trading.[2] It also outlined how the index-based derivative market in India has outpaced all other stock markets across the globe combined.

What exactly is index-based derivative trading?

In the simplest terms, you know there are various companies that are listed in any stock market. These come from sectors or industries based on their product or service. Some of these may include IT, automobiles, chemicals, textiles, energy and so on. An index is basically an indicator of how a particular market as a whole, or any specific sector, is performing. The computation of this indicator is based on statistical calculation and in general if the value of this indicator (or index) is rising, it is seen as a positive sign for the sector or the market in general.

Index-based derivative trading is seen as a trading format where different types of traders (retail, institutional, foreign, etc.) place their trades on the direction (up or down) this index will go towards, and with how much momentum. This trading happens over something called option contracts and each contract has a minimum trading amount that needs to be paid as a premium when being bought. Sensex and Midcap-Nifty are examples of such indices. The Sensex is an index of 30 BSE-listed companies across different sectors, and the Midcap-Nifty is an index of 150 companies listed on the NSE ranking from 101 to 250.

Having said all this, the report by Axis Mutual Fund does not view index-based trading with a positive outlook for retail traders. It talks about how the chances of making money in fantasy games are much higher as compared to index-based

---

[2]Gupta, Ashish, 'ACUMEN: "Gamification" of Indian Equities', Axis Mutual Fund, 30 September 2023, https://tinyurl.com/3mfumf44. Accessed on 3 March 2025.

derivatives trading.

For people who don't understand hedging, it's basically a strategy to mitigate losses. To offset the market conditions that go opposite to an initial view, investors and traders generally place counter-trades on the same security to lower the potential losses from the main trade.

~ 50% of options traded on expiry day

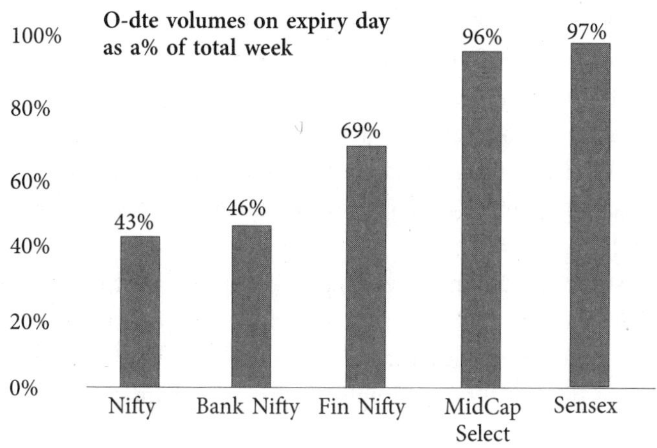

Source: NSE, BSE, Axis, MF Research Data as on 31 July 2023

The graph above is till 31 July 2023 and gives an idea of the volume of index-based derivative trading on their respective expiry days. As you can see, most of the trading in the Sensex and Midcap-Nifty is happening on the expiry day. This data for the rest of the indices has also changed since then. Thus, the concept of hedging, for which the option contracts were really designed, is not really applicable anymore.

What does this mean?

It simply means that traders in derivatives are mostly coming to the stock market for the kick, for an adrenaline rush equal to that of a sports betting app. The sole intent here is to trade only on the expiry day as most of the volatility and liquidity happen then. The chance of making or losing money is also at its peak then.

Young traders are more than happy to pay for information on what to buy, when to buy and when to exit. With this, they inadvertently open themselves up to a world of scamsters who are waiting to pounce on gullible and greedy folks to sell the exact same courses, live calls and private sessions.

Stock market fraud has always existed and will always exist in some form or the other. Theft can't be stopped completely. On the same note, even regulators can only go so far to stop fraud. What can really be done is to focus on reality and detach from dreams. This is how you, who are reading this, can protect yourself.

As we were talking earlier, there is a dark aspect to the stock market. We can call them the 'drugs of the stock market'. The ones people get addicted to.

Let's discuss them at length in the next chapter.

2

ARE STOCK MARKET TIPS EQUIVALENT TO DRUGS?

'Hey dude, try this out. It is the next level of ecstasy. You will feel out of this world!' A college senior, Sanjay (name changed), told me at one of our college events.

'No! I am not interested. But…th…thanks!' I ran away before I even completed my sentence.

Sanjay offered the same 'ecstasy' to 30 other students that night—I am sure at least a few tried it.

Sanjay made some money at every such event night, from people who tried the 'ecstasy' and then paid for more. Three years later, Sanjay was still struggling with his degree but was making a decent income supplying ecstasy to college students. This is how even a couple of my friends ended up in rehab. Last I heard, Sanjay had become a local corporator and was working with a few local corrupt politicians. His wife and son had left him a few years back. I felt bad for him.

The Trap

A decade later, I was sitting in my office. My phone rang. The voice on the other end said, 'Hello, sir. I am Rakesh from "Instant Rich Tips" based out of Indore. I am a senior advisory counsellor. Sir, do you trade in the stock market?'

'Yes, sometimes. Why?' I responded.

'Sir, I would like to offer you a trial tips plan and we can get you 20 per cent to 30 per cent profit on a daily basis. If you like the plan, I can tell you the pricing next time. What do you think?'

'No. I am not interested. I learn and trade on my own,' I said.

'Sir, here is what I am telling you. I will give you buying levels with stop-loss and a target price. If you make a profit, I will tell you about the plans we have and even offer a discount. Doesn't this seem correct to you?' he tried again.

Before I complete the story, let me tell you what these technical terms mean.

A stock market tip such as this one comes with three price points. One is the entry price. At this price, one generally buys the share. Then, there are two exit prices. The share, post your buy, may either go up or drop in value. If the share price drops, you are given a stop-loss based on the maximum loss one takes. If the price goes up, a target price is provided which is basically another exit but in profit this time.

So, for instance, if you get a stock market tip that says buy xyz share at 100, target 125, stop-loss 90, which basically means that if you purchase the share at 100 and it sees a drop of 90 or hits a value of 125, you must exit. Else you keep your position open either way till any of these price points is reached.

And now back to the story. I cut the call and went back to my work.

Let's say such a call goes to 100 people every day by every such 'senior advisory counsellor'. How many will say 'yes' and how many will respond the way I did? Well, it depends on the leads, the calling script, the confidence of the caller, and so on. In general, let's say 40 people. Filtering out the 10 per cent of genuine advisories out there (my approximate calculation based on my years of research and study of the space in India, especially Indore), there is a specific modus operandi. As an aside, I love Indore—it's a beautiful city with amazing people sans this advisory part.

What would Rakesh, the guy from that advisory, do? He will first pick up a stock or get a stock picked up from the 'advisors' inside his company. Then he will do something really obnoxious.

Out of the 40 people who said yes to him, he tells 20 to buy the stock and 20 to sell it.

What do you think is going to happen?

Well, the trial tip will work for at least one set of 20 people. Nobody, including Rakesh, knows which set. Those 20 people will see a small profit in their account. This is new money they did not have to work for. Rakesh helped them get it. He is a saviour, a messiah! All these 20 people now love Rakesh.

What will they do next? Most of them will call Rakesh and ask for the plan he has to offer. He will happily offer multiple plans and will not negotiate at all. A decent percentage of those 20 people will be converted to paid clients.

Now, I'm sure you remember how the tip was created in the first place. If Rakesh is a serious scamming professional, he will still call the other set of 20 people who lost money and apologize to them. These 20 people despise him because they lost money due to him. To them Rakesh is nothing less than a conman.

This is what that call will sound like.

'Hello, sir. I am so sorry. Our advisory recommendations mostly work but that day the market took a sudden unanticipated move. You will be happy to know that we had given a fairly small stop-loss. I have heard a lot of people lost huge chunks of their money.'

Some of those vulnerable people might still be listening to Rakesh.

'Sir, this is what I offer. I give you another trial tip for free. This time you put a smaller amount. Just see the percentage of return this tip will give you. After that I will even get you a 30 per cent discount. What do you say?'

If you could see Rakesh at this point, you would see someone with their fingers crossed as they take a shot in the dark with minimal expectations but definite possibilities.

Some of the loss-making traders will still say yes to this call. Basically, clients who considered Rakesh to be a messiah got no discount, while the others got a 30 per cent discount on the same plan. This is the plan—and this is how Rakesh makes money.

This was just one example. But Rakesh and Sanjay are the same person. They are ruining the world without caring for the repercussions of their professions.

The Modus Operandi

Isn't that a bit extreme?

Some of you might be thinking that, about that prior statement.

No, it's not extreme and I will explain how. My friends who ended up taking drugs and ruining their health consistently were on the same tangent as those who kept calling Rakesh for tips and plans. They always crave more.

Now, let's focus on these 'tips' businesses. The modus operandi of Rakesh's company is pretty much how today's Telegram channels or some finance influencers across social media operate. Getting lucky with a tip encourages greed and then people run to tip providers with their wallets open, asking for more.

Things change once you actually buy such a plan. You will get their 'service'. A few of those tips will keep working while the rest won't. When you lose money and you call 'Rakesh', he will say the same thing he said to the other loss-making traders. This will go on for a while until you exhaust your capital or mental peace, or both. Then one day, the sun will glow with some energy that will strike the rational part of your brain and you will ask yourself, 'What the hell am I even doing?'

In most cases, this will come pretty late after a lot of losses. However, if you are lucky enough to get that dose early, then congratulate yourself and move on.

(De)-Addiction

As with drugs, taking tips and trading based on these becomes nothing less than an addiction. There is a dopamine effect. As per the National Institute of Drug Abuse in India (NIDA), the dopamine signal causes changes in neural connectivity that make it easier to repeat the activity without thinking about it, leading to the formation of habits. One becomes anxious and depressed when deprived of these substances. Then it becomes hard to think or focus on anything else. It's a temporary high, but it's a high nonetheless.

Withdrawals from either are not easy. Your social behaviour and your treatment of money see a significant change. If challenged about usage, you get aggressive. That's a classic addiction.

This addiction can stop at a relatively early stage for those who use rationality in what is going on with them. But for the majority, it only ends when they have nothing else left to sell. I have seen people stealing money from their own houses, taking loans from friends and relatives, taking personal loans, and in some cases, even selling their property.

Just to get that one next best trade.

This works the worst for those who have seen these gimmick tips working for them. These people unfortunately see a lot of cash in their accounts thanks to these tips. That's why they bring in more money.

Drugs take away your health, your life goals and vision. Trading tips do the same, it's just that the realization comes much later.

So, what is the solution?

There is no pill or injection that can make a drug addiction go away, there is only rehabilitation. Similarly, there is no solution or advice to get out of an addiction to tips. I mean, the solution is not to take them in the first place.

How do you avoid the addiction?

Think rationally

There is no shortcut to anything made particularly for your benefit. It's always just for the one selling it.

For starters, block any of the phone calls or text messages you get from any advisors. Do not talk to or respond to them. They are trained to break your logic towards the market. They will paint you an unrealistic picture and this is how they earn their salaries. So just ignore the calls.

Uninstall Telegram if you are into trading

If someone calls you one day and says, 'Sir, I have something to show you. Come, have a look. I won't sell you anything,' the caller is right. He won't sell you anything because there is no need for it. Human nature is such that you won't stop at looking and you will want to go beyond. Your logic will go to sleep for an unknown period, and you will buy the scam on your own.

The better option is not to look. Never agree to what the caller says. Never pick up the call in the first place. Having said that, Telegram as an app has a huge potential to work for those who use it, but in the context of the Indian stock market, it is just being abused.

Uninstall the app.

Ask for your 'SEBI-registered' broker/advisor's licence number

Always check the licence details on SEBI's website. Even if you search for the keyword 'SEBI Registered Research Analysts' or 'SEBI Registered Investment Advisors' or 'SEBI Registered Portfolio Managers', you will reach a link where you can search for the validity details of the person reaching out to you. If you really want to trade on the basis of trading tips (since you don't have time left from your job or business), check the authenticity of the person providing the tips.

However, remember that getting tips from a SEBI-registered entity is NOT a guarantee of making profits either. They are just legal providers of the same tips. It's as good as the drug that is allowed under limited usage by the government for medical purposes. Even SEBI-registered tip providers cannot, by law, induce you to trade more or trade in the stocks that they themselves are trading in. Even if you are taking a legal tip, ideally you must validate the first few and then keep doing the same randomly.

How do you validate?

Apply some simple stock market basic analysis on the recommendations being made. Unlike Telegram-based or unregistered advisors, SEBI-registered advisors are supposed to provide you with the recommendation report of the tip they have given to you. You must read that report. Ask some questions. Get your doubts cleared.

If you are putting your hard-earned money into the stock market based on someone else's recommendation, you still need to know the basics of trading and market analysis. You can't have zero idea about stock market trading and still expect to make a decent return.

I guess you got the point.

But do you know what really happens inside these shady Telegram channels, especially the ones without any SEBI licences?

Let's discuss this in the next chapter.

Part 2

SOCIAL MEDIA SCAMS

3

REALITY OF TELEGRAM CHANNELS (WITHOUT SEBI LICENCE)

The Indian stock market, like any other global stock market, has seen its fair share of frauds and scams. Most of these have happened and continue to happen in the name of the stock market without any direct or indirect connection with the regulator or the regulated entities.

Let me walk you through this.

There was a time when people put funds in their trading accounts and got defrauded. There were instances of fraud where the broker placed buy and sell through those trading accounts without the client knowing. This still happens but the frequency has reduced.

Then came the era of stock market advisors based out of Indore, Mumbai and Gujarat. They made a lot of money by calling people on their cell phones and selling them different kinds of trading plans ranging from ₹2,000 to ₹10 lakh. As expected, most of these people were not registered with SEBI. While these practices are still in play, new-age traders are now getting defrauded on social media.

The king of social media where all sorts of stock market frauds eventually take place is Telegram.

Telegram is a safe haven for stock market fraudsters as it does not open any personal or contact info except a Telegram ID.

Hundreds and thousands of users can be added to channels where the audience can only react with an emoji. Only the group admin talks in such Telegram channels. It's a mute audience with any distraction being buried.

How are these fraudsters getting their audience?

The answer is quite simple. A lot of the user base is brought to Telegram by a social media profile. It could be a YouTube channel, an Instagram profile or an X (earlier Twitter) page. First, everyone is brought to a free Telegram channel and then from there paid audiences are funnelled to a different 'premium' Telegram channel.

Now the question is: what happens there? Scams of different varieties and flavours.

Unregistered Advisory and Tips

Telegram and WhatsApp are full of hundreds of channels with an audience base of a few thousand to a lakh users. There are filled with profit screenshots which are floated around along with trading levels for free. Buy this, sell here; sell this, buy there.

The goal is to entice the audience as the basic modus operandi. Once a portion of the audience starts getting mesmerized by all the money (or the depiction of it via profit screenshots) shown, they are lured into a paid channel with paid plans.

All these screenshots are just the tip of the iceberg. There are thousands of these shared every single day. Nothing works better than these screenshots to expose the greed of budding traders.

Let's talk more about this greed.

It's not complicated. Money drives greed and they start believing what they are seeing (or are shown). They want it to be true and sooner or later they give in to their desires. Most of these people are not willing to learn the concepts of the stock market or have already lost money while trading.

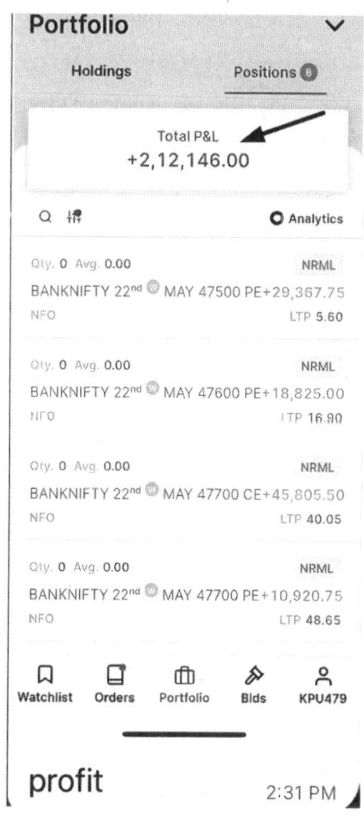

They don't just waste money by paying these Telegram channels; they also lose huge capital amounts in trading using the tips given in these channels.

How are these tips generated?

I will explain this using an example.

Meet Suresh. He runs one such Telegram channel. His business idea is simple. He asks for ₹5,000 for a paid monthly subscription in which he provides two-three daily option tips. Every month about 200 users pay him and he makes ₹10 lakh for the month.

Simple, right?

But there is just one problem. Suresh does not know anything about option trading. He tried it himself and lost ₹3 lakh. He is just making up a tip every day and sharing opposite positions to each half of his user base. This means half his users are being suggested an upside and half are getting a downside.

Suresh also subscribes to other known Telegram channels and copies its tips to later forward to his subscribers. This is also Suresh's seventh Telegram channel. The other six have been closed down as they were reported by subscribers or went into a loss.

In the next three months, Suresh plans to buy a 3-BHK in a posh colony of the town. He says thank you and thinks he has made it in life.

How to Recognize Such Channels?

One easy way to spot these is that the description says: 'We are not SEBI-registered. Tips provided are for educational purposes only.' But you need to know that if they take any consideration (cash or non-cash) from anyone in lieu of these tips, it is illegal. Plus, the tips in these channels are followed by emojis of fire, rockets, roses and more.

Have you watched the movie *Hera Pheri 2*? There was a character offering a 'Laxmi Chit-fund' and telling people they will double their investment amount in 25 days.

However, most chit-funds, either in the movie or in general, are cheat-funds. Telegram is full of such people shouting:

- Bring 10,000 and take 40,000 in 2 hours
- Bring 15,000 and take 60,000 in 3 hours
- Bring 20,000 and take 80,000 in 2 hours
- Bring 100,000 and take 400,000 in 12 hours

Check this:

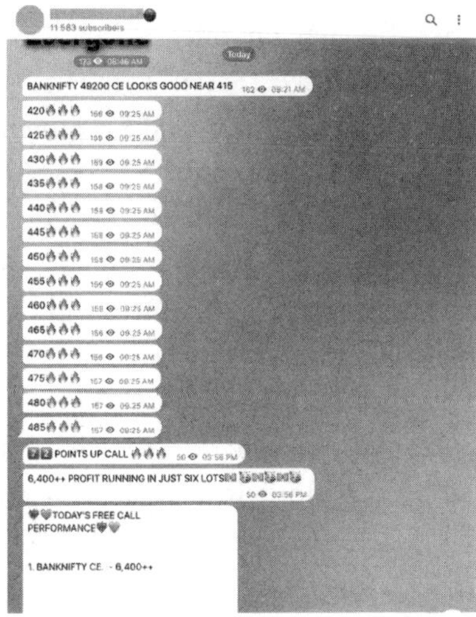
11 583 subscribers
Today
BANKNIFTY 49200 CE LOOKS GOOD NEAR 415
420
425
430
435
440
445
450
455
460
465
470
475
480
485
POINTS UP CALL
6,400++ PROFIT RUNNING IN JUST SIX LOTS
TODAY'S FREE CALL PERFORMANCE
1. BANKNIFTY CE - 6,400++

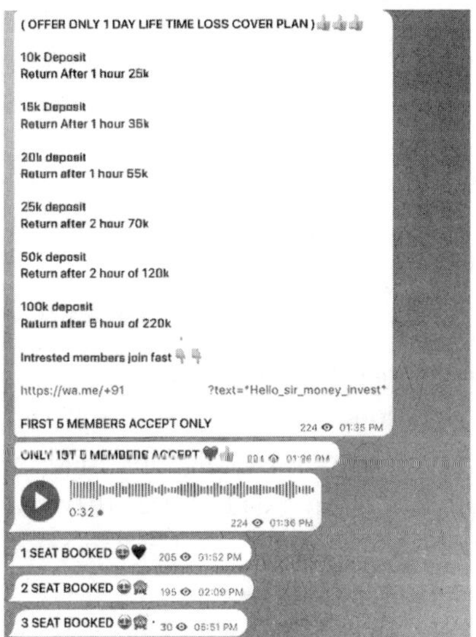
(OFFER ONLY 1 DAY LIFE TIME LOSS COVER PLAN)
10k Deposit
Return After 1 hour 25k
15k Deposit
Return After 1 hour 35k
20k deposit
Return after 1 hour 55k
25k deposit
Return after 2 hour 70k
50k deposit
Return after 2 hour of 120k
100k deposit
Return after 5 hour of 220k
Intrested members join fast
https://wa.me/+91 ?text="Hello_sir_money_invest"
FIRST 5 MEMBERS ACCEPT ONLY
224 01:35 PM
0:32
224 01:36 PM
1 SEAT BOOKED
205 01:52 PM
2 SEAT BOOKED
195 02:09 PM
3 SEAT BOOKED
30 06:51 PM

You may wonder who would pay these amounts and does any of this really work?

When you ask the person offering all this, they say, 'All these funds are collectively traded through an institutional trading account in the derivatives and crypto market. Specific cryptocurrencies are picked that are relatively volatile and there is movement in them. We, as a fund, make a decent percentage but return only 400 per cent. We keep the rest as a fee.'

So yes, a lot of people do end up paying these Telegram channels only to find themselves blocked from the group as soon as the payment is made. One may ask this question: if these channels can make 400 per cent to 500 per cent returns, why don't the channel owners do it with their own money?

Account-Handling Services

This is another type of service you can get on Telegram, eventually to get scammed. A Telegram channel will tell you:

- Minimum capital: ₹4–5 lakh
- 50–50 per cent sharing
- 20 per cent to 30 per cent daily expected profit
- Regular profit sharing
- Broker ID/password must be shared with OTP sign-in

Don't you smell something fishy already?

Firstly, as mentioned in the double-triple profit scam, why are these Telegram channels asking for funds when they can make 20 to 30 per cent on a daily basis. They can do it on their own and if they are so confident about their profits, they can even take a loan from the bank.

Secondly, this is illegal. In official terms, there is no service called account handling. There are portfolio management services (PMS) under SEBI Regulations 2020, which requires anyone managing a portfolio to have a PMS licence.

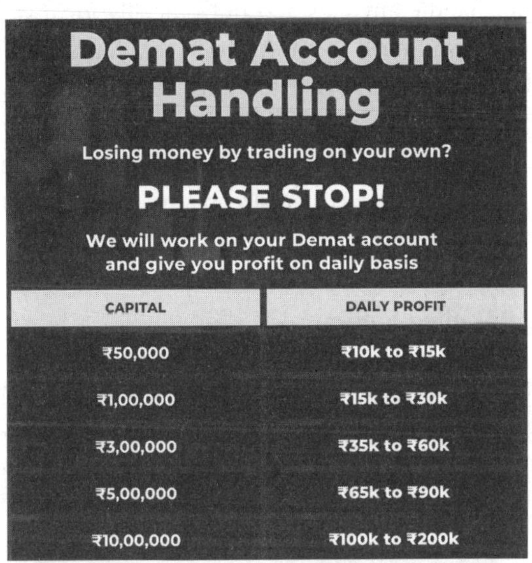

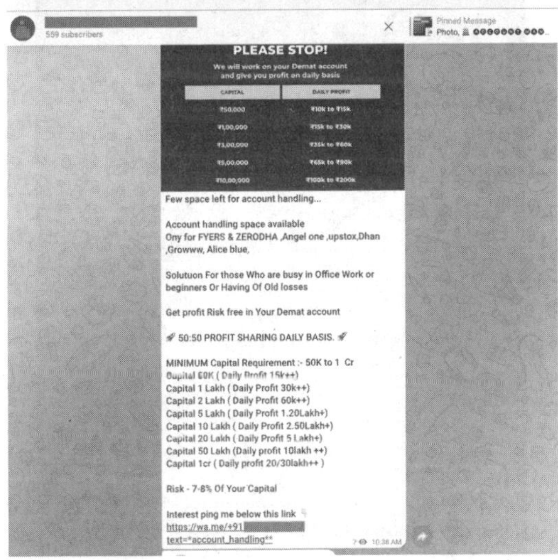

Furthermore, the minimum ticket size for managing funds through mainstream portfolio management services is ₹50 lakh. You cannot handle anyone's account officially for less than that amount. Also, you need to pay ₹10–15 lakh yourself to be called a portfolio manager, and that too after clearing all the requisite exams.

Therefore, the shady account handling and management services you see on Telegram are scams and eventually dupe the person opting in.

Fake Algo-Trading Software

The next type of scam is the 'fake algo-trading software scam' where you are asked for money in lieu of an algo-trading setup that always makes money. Here are a couple of such shady algo software:

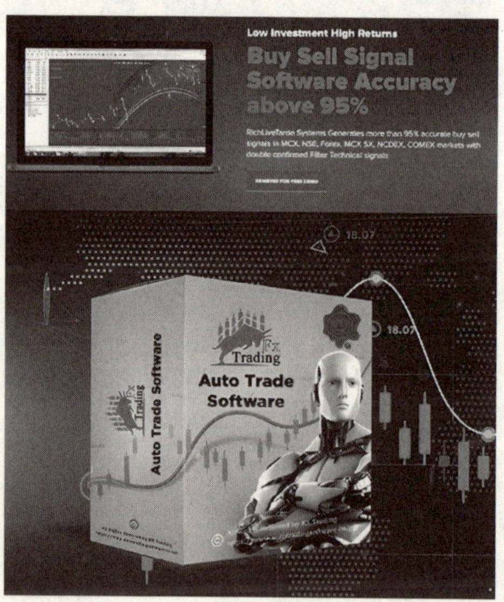

You are told that this system never loses money, that there are almost no draw-downs.

Here is the pitch: This so-called bullet-proof algo software has been tested for the last 20 years of data and inherits all sorts of market movements and situations. It knows how to react to what kind of move the market makes at any given point in time. You are told not to worry. Just keep putting in capital and see the magic happen where this algo-solution gives you multi-fold returns. There will be:

- Automatic entry, exits
- Auto setting of stop-loss and target price
- In-built risk-reward management

This software will give you one trending stock every day and you can capture profit every day in 15–20 minutes. You can get 200 to 300 points on an everyday basis!

Honestly, if this were all true, it would just take a few days for anyone to beat Elon Musk or Bernard Arnault based on the capital amount deployed. Heck, even Mansa Musa, the richest person ever on the planet, is not a far-off target from these standards.

All this is a gimmick to get you to buy this useless product made by some random scamsters.

You are better off without them.

With the latest SEBI circular in place, it has become much simpler for anyone to figure out a fake algo-trading software from a real one. The SEBI circular now states that if someone sells an algo-trading software without open code, a SEBI Research Analyst (RA) licence is mandatory.

Basically, if someone sells you this kind of algo-trading software, ask for the SEBI RA registration number and validate it on the SEBI website.

The Problem with These Telegram Channels

These are not SEBI-registered people. This implies no one has done a background verification on their education, qualification, experience and so on. They have not taken any exam that validates them as a person or entity who is eligible to provide such tips. This means it is tough to know whether they are even technically good enough to provide these tips.

There are no regulations or bindings on these individuals. They can do anything and everything under the sun. Unlike a SEBI-registered IA or RA, they don't have anything at stake and nothing to lose. If one Telegram channel gets blocked someday, they will open another one.

If you end up making a loss from these channels, there is nothing much you can do against them as the SEBI complaints portal won't allow you to file a complaint. You can send an email to sebi@sebi.gov.in, but it is the regulator's discretion whether to take action or issue an advisory or warning against the person.

None of these folks have done much in their own stock market trading journey. They are neither authorized nor have been able to prove themselves profitable in any format. So, if you end up paying to any of these scams, you help the ecosystem grow even further and open the door for future scamsters to trap new gullible traders.

The worst part is that those who lose money due to these channels do not speak about it. They are afraid that if they tell the world they were scammed online by people they don't even know, they will be laughed at. Thus, awareness around such scams is not widespread.

Simply speaking, keep your emotions intact. Nothing is ever as easy as it is shown in the stock market. It is as difficult an industry to make money from, as any other industry is.

Moving on to another app that's used even more than Telegram—a messaging app that almost 50 crore Indians use regularly.

WhatsApp!

But why are we talking about WhatsApp in the context of stock market scams? Did you know there is fraud happening in the name of the stock market on this app also? In fact, the scale of these frauds is in crores.

I investigated one such scam by becoming a client. More in the next chapter.

4

HOW TO SAVE YOURSELF FROM A WHATSAPP GROUP FRAUD

'Hear me out. I've gotten into stock market investments! I thought I would invest in stocks by learning about them but it seems I have the stars in my favour. Yesterday I was added by someone into a JPMorgan WhatsApp group and it seems legit, bro.'

This is what my friend Varun told me in a single breath when he called me some time ago.

'They also sent me a presentation and gave me a one-to-one session,' Varun continued.

'Okay, what else did they say?' I asked, curious.

'There is a professional lady from their end. What was her name? Umm…yeah Ishita… Ishita Shenoy. She sent me a plan that showed potentially huge profits. They say they work in the Indian stock market directly with companies and know the ins and outs of what is going on, as well as which stocks specifically are going to see a jump,' Varun responded.

'That's great! But that's impossible, and even if it isn't so, it is illegal,' I said, with a bit of sarcasm.

'What? But she said this is a closed group of large investors,' he continued trying to convince me.

'Sure. Answer a few questions for me,' I asked seriously.

'Okay…,' he prepared himself and sat up straighter.

'Why did they add YOU? How did they get your number? Why are they doing it with normal people with relatively smaller amounts of money as compared to corporates? Big companies have big money, so they can directly convince them instead, right? What do you think?' I asked.

I think he wanted to say something else but this is what he said, 'Got it. Thank you.'

A few days later, he called to tell me that a couple of users from that same WhatsApp group lost in excess of ₹50 lakh and ₹2 crore worth of capital respectively. It even appeared in the newspaper a few days later.

Stock Market Frauds: WhatsApp Edition

This is not an isolated case. In fact, there are many. Just go to Google and search 'WhatsApp stock market frauds India'.

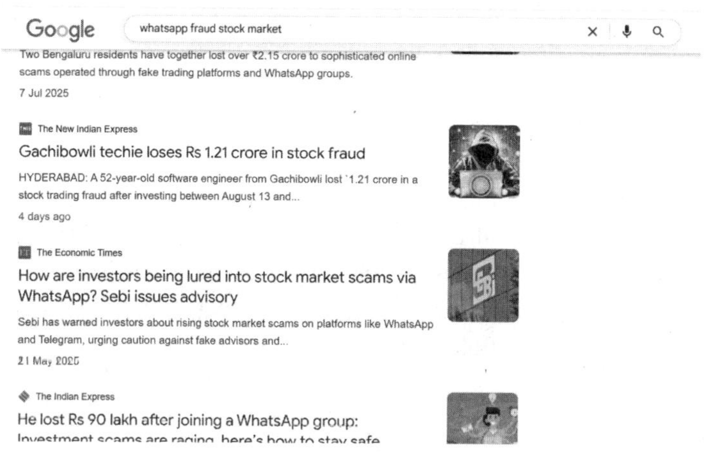

Okay, here is another one. Search for: 'WhatsApp trading scam crores'.

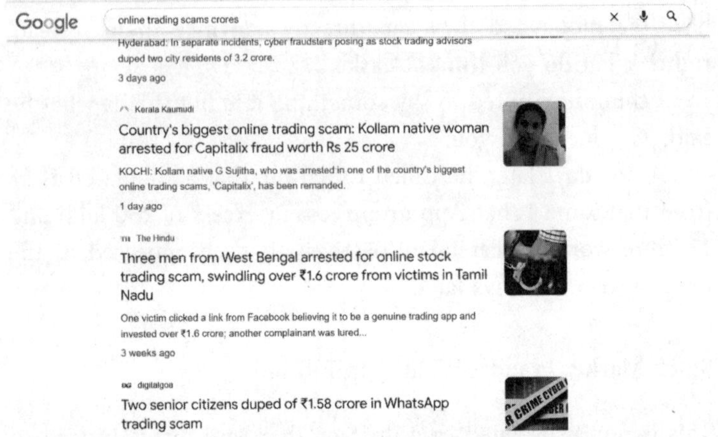

You can keep searching for similar keywords and you will keep finding multiple stories of scams happening all around the country. It's strange how never ending it all is.

People keep falling prey to these scams and it's not that the victims are uneducated or have a limited technical understanding of such worldly affairs. On the contrary, most of these victims are businesspeople, doctors, software engineers, retired teachers and government employees. They still end up becoming prey to these scammers who have a pretty basic modus operandi. One only needs to use basic common sense to understand all this.

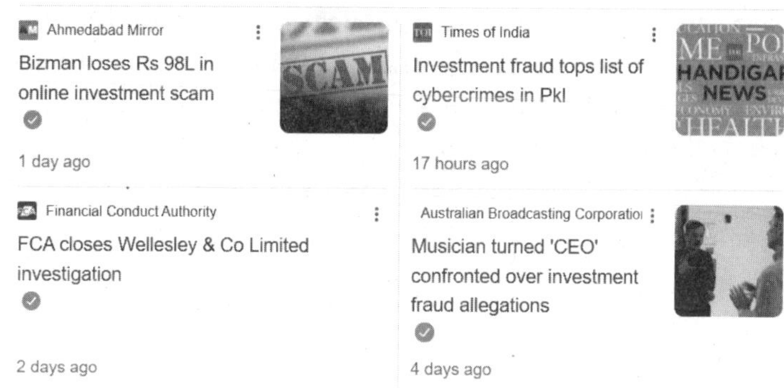

Furthermore, the scale of these scams is not just a few thousands or lakhs but in higher multiples of crores of rupees every time. Interestingly, a major chunk of victims do not even come out to say that they have been robbed of their money. They don't want to lose social respect and asked how they could be so gullible. Such discussions end within the hearts of the victims or at best within the conversations of the families.

What, Why, and How?

What exactly is this fraud and how do they loot people?

It all starts with an advertisement, either on Facebook or Instagram. Once you click on this ad, you reach a WhatsApp group. The name may have a big brand mentioned in it. Some examples are: JP Morgan, Vijay Kedia, Jefferies Investing, Rekha Jhunjhunwala, or any names in the corporate or personal brand space within finance and investments. Some ads even use social media finfluencers, or financial influencers, who have a credible reputation.

Now these scamsters are using high-class names that are known to mostly urban residents. This also implies they expect the victim to be educated. An educated victim living in an urban city will have more money, generally speaking. Now, once people get added to a WhatsApp or a Telegram group, this is what they see as the welcome message:

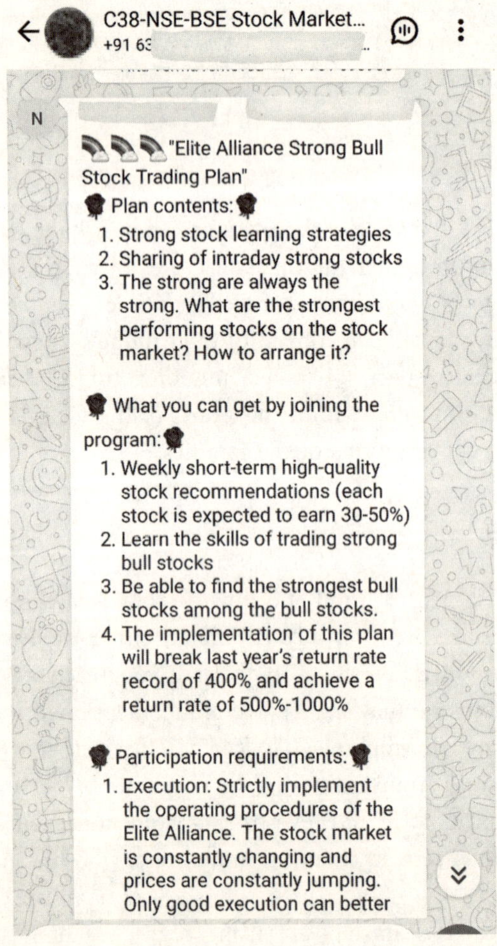

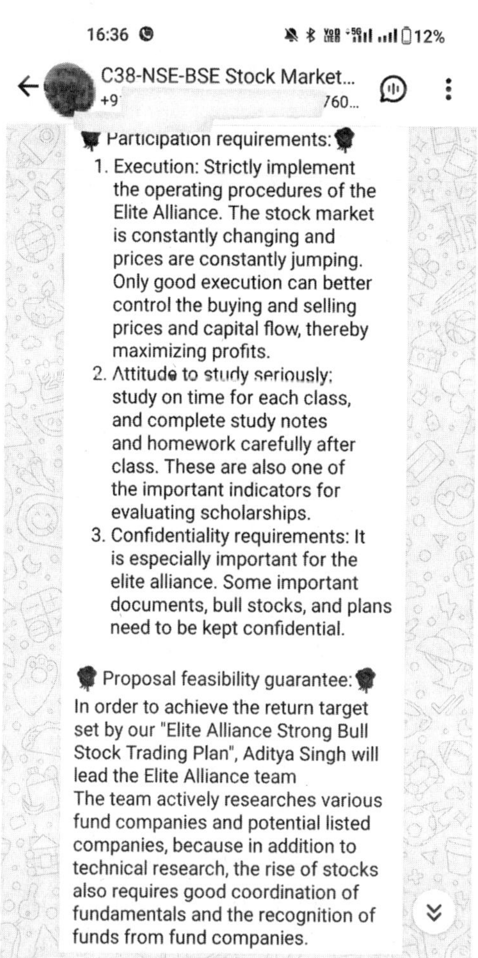

The language in this welcome message contains keywords such as strategies, intraday strong stocks, bull market and so on. This sets the user up to believe this is a highly sophisticated group with financial content. Generally, the flavour of the language is so fancy that it seems outside the reach of a usual resident.

How do they entice people?

By using engaging phrases such as:

> 'Each stock is expected to earn 30–50per cent.'
>
> 'The implementation of this plan will break last year's return rate record of 400 per cent and achieve a return rate of 500 per cent–1,000 per cent.'

Why do people think that this can actually work in their favour?

In this message, there is a person 'Aditya Singh' (there is always such a name) who is positioned as someone who is high up in the stock-market investing space. He is going to 'personally' attend to and assist everyone in the WhatsApp group to make a lot of money. In fact, private consultations are also available.

Friends, let me tell you one thing that I am sure of. We do a lot of ground research where we go to towns and villages to try to glean the depth of understanding people have about the stock market. We try to find out how they perceive the market and whether they know entities such as stockbrokers, SEBI, NSE and so on. What we have learned is that urban audiences are usually aware of such things.

Why wouldn't they be?

A fair chunk of people in an urban setting are more likely to be educated, speak English professionally, and make a decent amount of money. So why wouldn't they know about SEBI, stockbrokers and so on. They would also know professionals need proper documentation and licences to practice, such as doctors, lawyers and chartered accountants.

Similarly, someone recommending stocks for investing in the market would also need a licence from a regulator of some sort. But that does not always seem to be true. If someone entices them with a Facebook or Instagram advertisement, gets them to join a WhatsApp group, and writes wonderfully crafted financial language, their vulnerabilities are exposed. They are okay to put in crores of rupees in a random account on the internet and expect that they will get 400 to 500 per cent returns. That implies they want their money to grow four to five times within a few months.

There are easily 200 to 400 members in these groups (apart from a mentor/professor/advisor and a moderator). All that these fraudsters expect is a two to three per cent conversion rate. As long as five to ten people end up paying a few lakhs to a few crores each, they are sorted. Once people are scammed, they are blocked from joining the group again.

Also, in any one such group, there are huge chances that 50 per cent to 60 per cent of the folks are from the fraudster's end. This is for the simple reason that the interaction level in a group like this needs to be high. It must seem that people are making money, are happy with the returns and love the mentor.

How do they make you give up your money?

I joined four to five of these groups and here are my observations. Once added to the group, I noticed a pattern: activities took place twice a day, once in the morning and then again in the evening. Each day began with a welcome message, followed by an exclusive 'tip', something supposedly known only to insiders. Often, it was linked to a stock undergoing a block trade—a situation where a large volume of shares was acquired by a big investor. The group provided a specific buying price, urging members to enter the trade immediately. Within minutes, an exit price was shared, usually showing a profit.

What followed was a flood of screenshots—traders flaunting massive earnings, some exceeding ₹40–50 lakh, creating an illusion of effortless wealth. The atmosphere was euphoric, filled with celebratory emojis and praises for the mentor, the group's central figure. As the session closed, the mentor shared a thank you note that was met with more admiration and promises of participation in the next trade.

Intrigued, I decided to test the waters. I simply typed 'I would like to try'. Within six minutes, an administrator messaged me privately. The conversation quickly escalated into a structured sales pitch filled with complex financial jargon and references to SEBI, all designed to create a sense of legitimacy. What followed was a shower of persuasion.

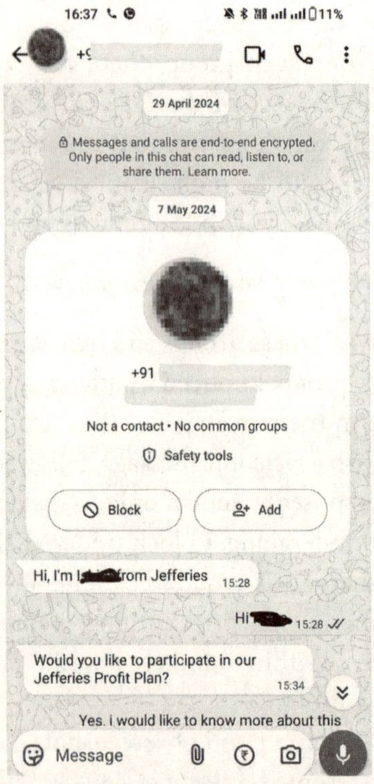

As far as I know, SEBI does not get into the fancy stuff mentioned in the presentation.

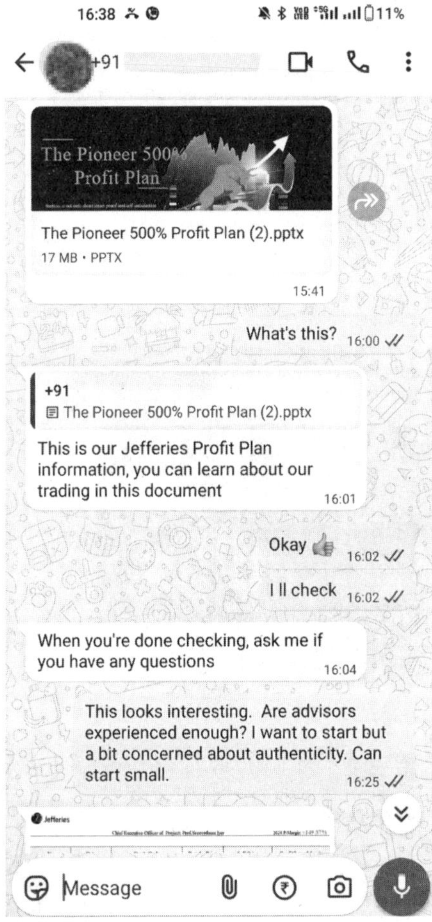

After the document was shared with me, I diluted my interest a bit because I wanted to see whether the person would follow up with me. The next morning, she did.

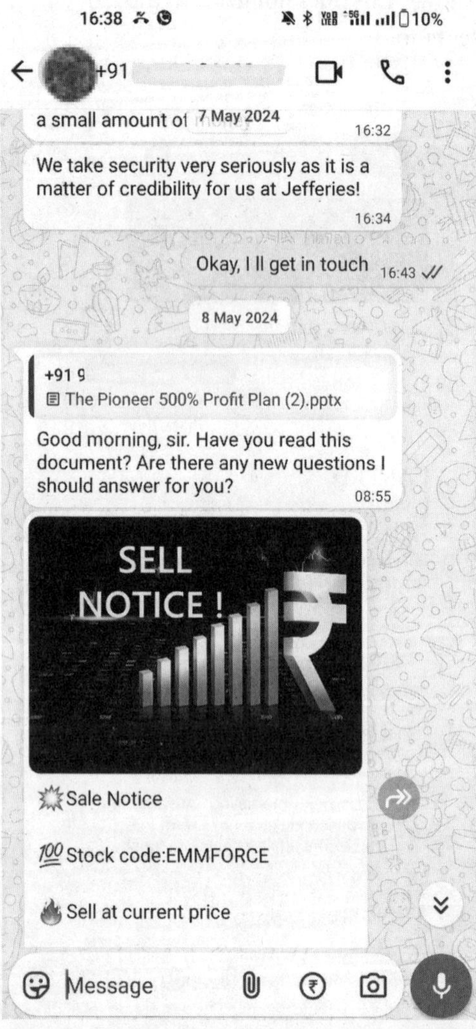

She went ahead and tried to lure me with tips. Some showed an expected profit percentage of 5 per cent, while others showed a 10 to 15 per cent profit in a day.

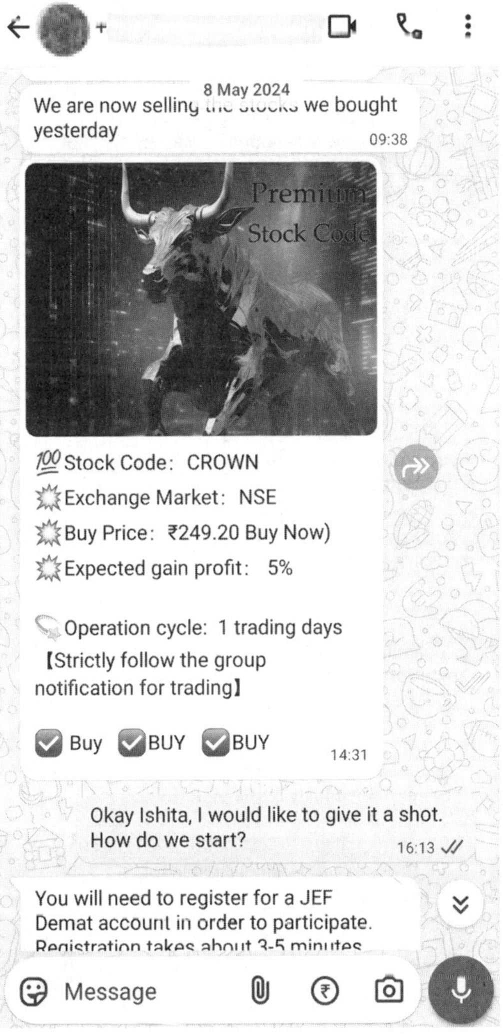

Next, I checked whether they were ready to answer a few relatively tough questions. I asked whether their advisors were authentic, trustable and experienced.

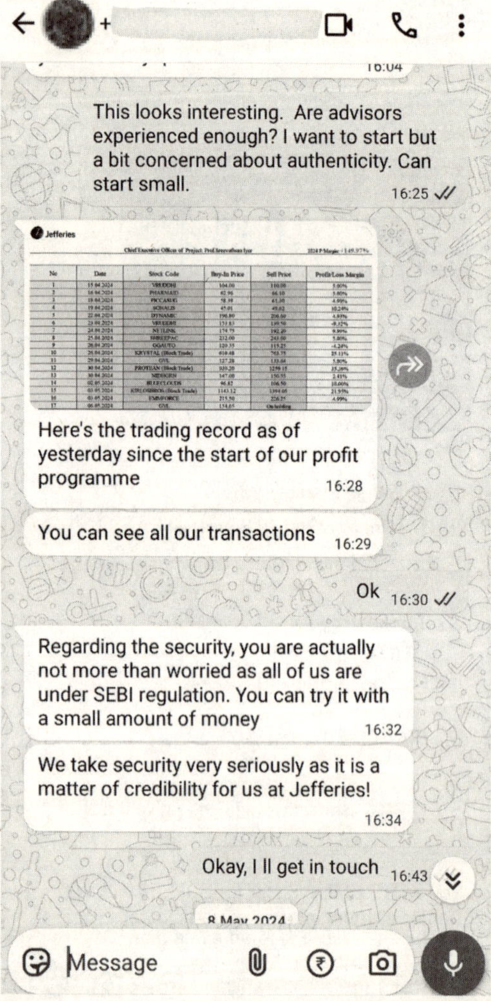

Once she knew that I was good to go, she shared the ace up her sleeve—the link to an application. Strangely enough, this app was hosted on the Google Play Store and had only 100+ installations.

Why do people still get taken in?

Well, there were 166 members in that WhatsApp group. I am pretty sure this was not their first one and these were not the only people that were part of such groups.

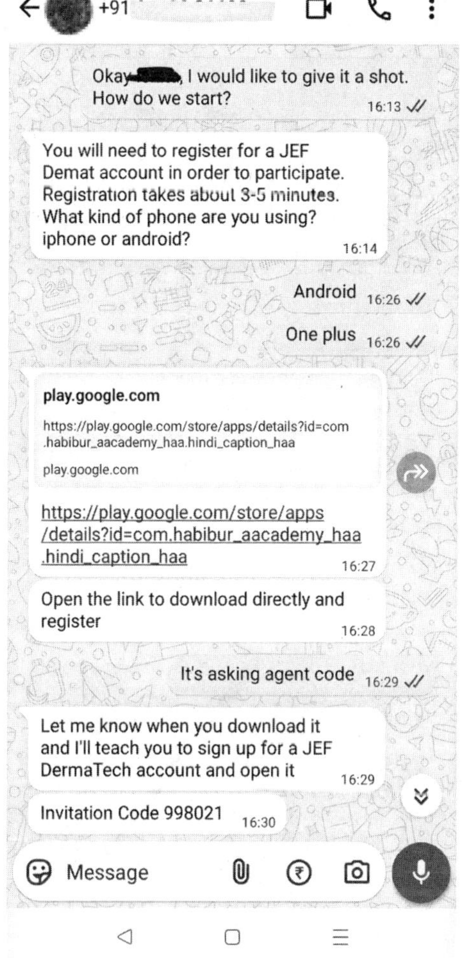

I installed the app with a bit of caution and fear. But the phone that I used for all this did not have any banking or payment app installed. So even if they could hack my phone, there was no financial information they would get their hands on.

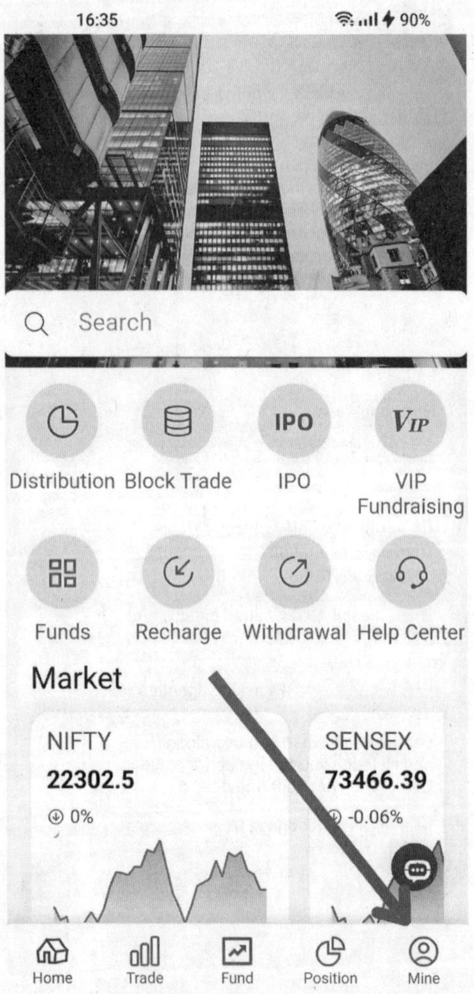

Look at this app. I ask again: how can people be so vulnerable that they can't differentiate between a valid trading app and this piece of whatever you would want to call it. Such an app can be developed for less than ₹20,000 in a span of 15–20 days by 1 or 2 developers.

Anyone who has used a trading app would know that this is nothing but a sham.

Next, I was told to do a KYC and put in the details of my bank account. I faked the details on both the screens and then I was asked by the person on the WhatsApp chat to contact the chat support of the application. They would assist me with the next steps of getting my trades done.

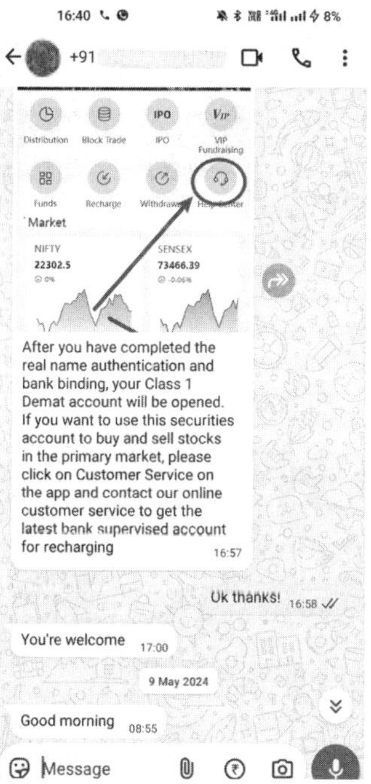

I did that. The chat support agent asked me the amount I would like to add. I said ₹50,000. I hope you're shocked to know that the person gave me the current- account details of a company based out of a second- or third-tier town called Bikaner in Rajasthan.

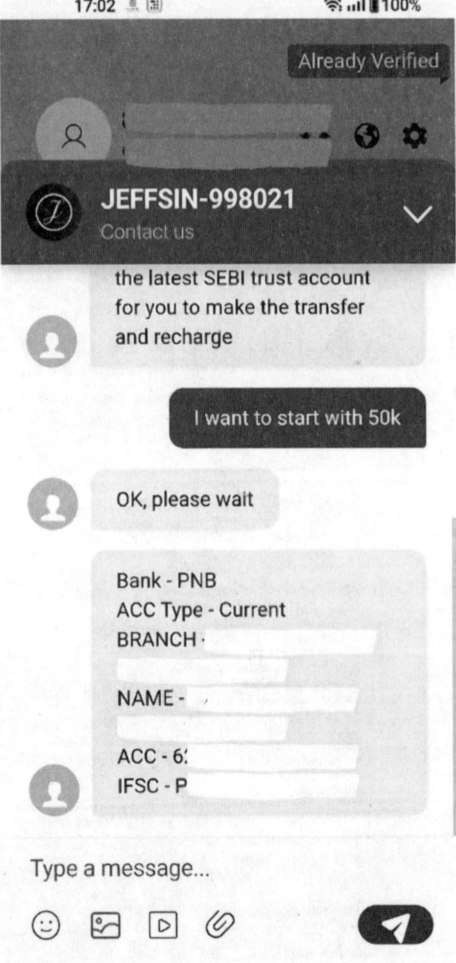

What happens next is up to what choice you make. A current account based in a small town should not be something that inspires confidence about making a transaction worth crores of rupees.

If you unfortunately agree to the next steps, all you are doing to yourself is bringing agony, loss of money, and a lot worse. You will start seeing profits in your demat. You will want to try taking out the money. Surprisingly, you may be able to withdraw money for the first or even second time. Then your greed will grow.

The next added amount will be a big one. You will start getting more excited seeing the monetary increase in your investment. You might want to withdraw some of that. But then something strange will happen. You will be asked to add more money in the form of a tax. You will do so.

Then you will try to withdraw the capital again. This time you will be asked to transfer 'transaction charges'. You will start feeling numb. You won't know what is happening. You could never have imagined this happening to you.

But, unfortunately, all of this is REAL.

You need to understand one thing. There is not even a one per cent chance that anyone in this world will add you to a random WhatsApp or Telegram group, start recommending stocks, and take care of your investments so that YOU can make money. I won't say that there is a 90 to 95 per cent chance that this is a scam. The possibility that this will end up in a scam is 100 per cent. So, the next time someone tries to lure you into such investments, block the group and move on.

In the next section, let's talk about another type of scam: trading apps. The kind that the stockbroker provides to place your trades.

5

CLONED TRADING APPS FRAUDS

'Which clone app do you want?'

'Which all do you have?'

'We have Zerodha, Angel One, Upstox. Which one do you want to buy?'

'I want Angel One. What features will I get?'

'Depends on the plan, here are the details: kite fake profit and loss app: ₹3,399 for full version, ₹5,599 for LTP version; Angel One: ₹8,599 for LTP version (online server), ₹6,299 for advanced version (offline server). So those who want to buy can contact us asap @xyz.'

'Why is the Angel One clone app so expensive?'

'Because we are the only ones who have been able to clone it. You won't get it anywhere else in the market. No traders know that there is a clone app of Angel One. All think it's just Zerodha.'

This is an excerpt from my discussion with a Telegram handle that sells clone trading applications. By the time you read this, there will be even more clone apps of Zerodha, Angel One, Groww and Finvasia in the Telegram 'market'. And like any other market, this also offers discounts.

You might be wondering what I am talking about.

My focus in this chapter is on fake or cloned versions of the trading apps that are spread across the trading community. In this kind of fraud, a clone app of a mainstream stockbroker is shown to the users on social media with ridiculous profit numbers.

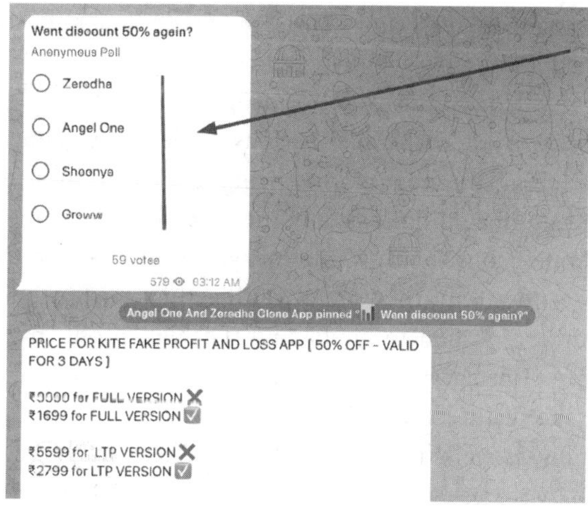

Who shows them and to whom are these shown?

New traders—i.e., beginners—believe what they see and assume the person showing them profits is actually making that much money. The ones with a sizeable social media following within the financial space and unethical intentions are the buyers of such clone trading apps. When someone sees such money being made, they first get attracted to the stock market and then get themselves enslaved to the person making the recommendation.

The 'investment' has been made by these influencers on these clone apps. Now it's time to get the return on investment (ROI). And how would that be done?

Simple. By making videos!

Before this, some configurational changes are made. These fake apps come with a backend so any random numbers can be added. The buy price, the sell price, quantity of securities or stocks, and even the profit values that the finfluencer wants to show off.

Then videos, reels and shorts are made and published on social media accounts for their followers.

These videos confuse a lot of people, attract a lot of people, and depress a lot of people. Serious traders feel demotivated when watching the huge profits being shown by these people. They end up imagining that only they are not able to make this much money consistently while everybody else is able to. New traders wonder why they aren't getting this much money and then they are pushed to contacting the high profit makers on Telegram or Instagram.

But the reality is different.

Nobody is really making any profits. These are just numbers added in by scamsters on clone trading apps. The numbers could be anything. These clone trading apps are connected to a server and thus, even if you refresh the screen, the numbers continue to seem as if they are on a real trading app.

How did we get here?

Basically, there is a market for fraudsters. This is for fraudsters selling to fraudsters to defraud the ones who want to get rich, the gullible, and the greedy. The most interesting part is that there are a few Telegram channels who don't even have a clone app to sell but they are faking to sell fake apps.

Fraudsters reach out to these fake Telegram channels asking for fake apps. The fake Telegram channel asks for a real payment at some point and then once the payment is made it blocks that fraudster from the channel. So, a fraudster who wants to defraud other people is defrauded by a fake Telegram channel selling fake trading apps.

With all this going around, the trading community is now filled with a lot of distrust. It is getting to the point where no one trusts anyone. This is both good and bad.

The ones who really want to learn doubt everyone and

they end up not learning stock market trading from anyone. Eventually, most of them lose out on their capital anyway by trading without learning. And the honest ones who really want to teach have a hard time making people believe in them.

Here is how this trust thing has shaped up:

There was a time when traders used to tweet or make a video saying 'I made ₹5 lakh in profit today.' Over time, people started doubting such claims. They tweeted back, 'We need to verify this. Post the screenshots.' Obviously, not all who were tweeting about their profits were honest. So the ones who were lying started editing loss-making screenshots to profit ones.

Some of these edited screenshots were caught and so were those scammers. With this, people then started doubting screenshots and started asking for screen recordings directly from the app. This was the point when some tech guy with a corrupt head on his shoulders thought of making a fake trading app. Now that people know that apps can also be cloned, they are asking for verified PnLs (profit and loss statements).

We are not far from the point when verified PnLs will also be faked.

Gosh!

This is excruciating but unfortunately true.

Who Makes These Apps? How Does Someone Get Access to Them?

Where there is a user base, there is a market, a grey one. There are tons of Telegram channels selling access to clone trading applications. Furthermore, these scamsters are not some uneducated folks. They talk about product features and offer multiple updates. They know what they are doing and have a plan.

Have a quick look at this screenshot:

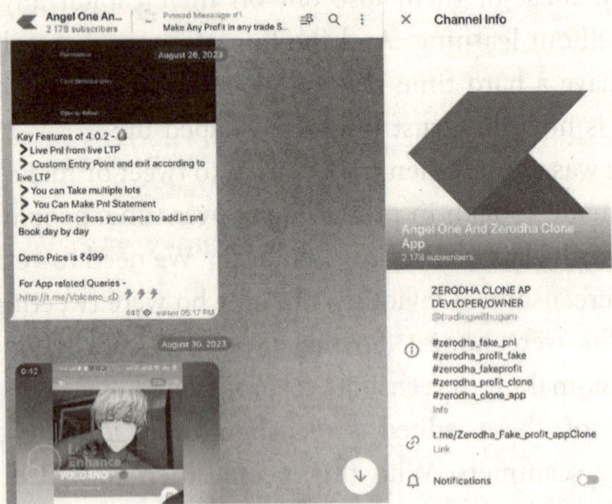

As mentioned earlier, there are different variants of clone apps as per the broker. Second, there is feature-based pricing. This is a black market functioning under the noses of the brokers and regulators. By the time such scams get the attention of the people who matter in the industry, lakhs of vulnerable retail traders would have become scapegoats.

The problem is not just limited to Telegram channels anymore. The confidence of such people has grown so much that there are exclusive websites selling fake apps. There is a website called 'zerodhaclone.com' which has a traffic base of 10,000 users a month. The website gives information on how the application works, what you really need to do to get it going, its different plans, and so on. It has an approved AdSense account and runs Google display ads.

Interestingly, there is an FAQ (frequently asked questions) section as well that talks about infringement, copyright and related legal issues with the usage of such an app. In a sense, the app warns users about how using it can harm them.

Here is how the website looks—an arms shop for stock market scammers.

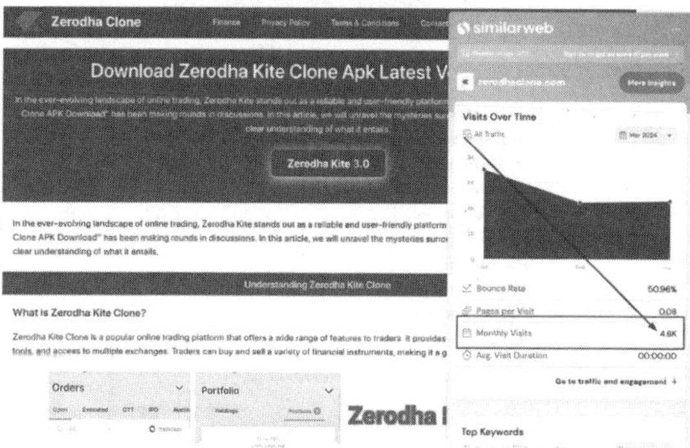

There are also people who search for such clone apps on Google for different brokers.

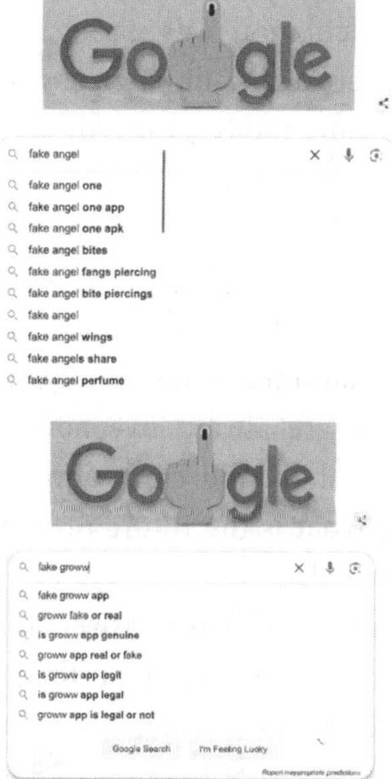

On top of all this, there are instances where influencers have been caught making silly mistakes on social media using these apps. There was one such example where the influencer forgot to add a "," between digits as it is shown in the original app. In another case, the calculation was wrong. One of the weirdest mistakes was one where a fake-finfluencer used Bank-Nifty index numbers while analysing the Nifty50. All of these influencers are trolled to this day.

As visible in this screenshot here, a fraudster had an MIS order position still open at 3:39 p.m. while the market automatically squares such a position at 3:30 p.m.

The thing with social media though is, if three people are criticizing you, there are always five new ones to fall in love with your fake screenshots and clone apps.

In this context, what is the future of all this and how will it impact retail traders?

This is something I don't have answers to, but if the regulator takes measures against such practices, then this would directly impact a lot of social media channels misusing such apps in order to fool people.

Will this ever end?

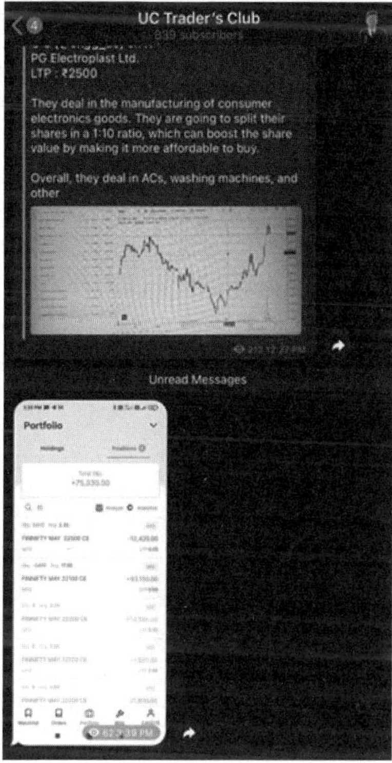

There is a likelihood of this happening but it will take time. In the interim, the scale of such scamsters is only going to increase and all you must do is not get (mis)influenced. This is all just a gimmick. The only thing you must do is to not get distracted by someone's profit screenshots, even if they are genuine.

Focus on the process of learning stock market concepts instead of chasing someone who can get you quicker glory because, as I have said before, the chances of that happening are close to negligible.

People may still succeed in distracting you with easy money. They offer you schemes where you don't have to do anything but put money in your trading account. No fees and no upfront costs. They will trade on your behalf and only take a cut from the profits.

But there is a problem.

What if your whole account gets blown up to zero?

6

PROFIT-SHARING SCAMS

Are you aware of people who 'help' people make profits on their capital and take a cut of that profit with no upfront costs?

Do you know this is just another scam called profit sharing? Read this:

Complaint 1

I am in big trouble because a guy named Ajitosh destroyed me. He took my demat account for account management and made very huge losses of ₹12 lakh. He started by making profits and took 40 per cent as a share, and after the huge losses he didn't return a single rupee and blocked me.

Please help me. I took loans for the recovery and I am in a huge trap. It is very difficult to manage. I am a middle-class guy.

Complaint 2

This is an account-handling service offered by a Telegram channel called MARKET MARVELS. I deposited ₹50,000 in my demat account and gave them my ID. The profit-sharing model was 50–50. The first day they showed a profit of ₹8,000 and I paid them ₹4,000.

The very next day, they blew through my entire

> capital of ₹50,000. Before my investment they said the maximum loss would be 5 per cent, but they just used the entire capital and didn't even set any stop-loss. I have tried to contact them but they avoid me.
>
> They're telling me to add more money and they will recover my loss. What shall I do?'

There are 500+ such messages and emails we have received in the last six months, around profit-sharing scams which look very lucrative at the onset but the climax is always, unlike in our Bollywood movies, a sad story.

Of course, sad for the victim, not for the scammer.

What Exactly Is a Profit-Sharing Scam?

In the clearest way possible, it is an arrangement between two greedy people. One who is greedy and dumb, while the other is greedy and cunning.

There are so many ways for a scamster to reach your pocket these days.

Honest people work hard to make money. One day they get a call from someone or they watch someone's reel or a video, or they join someone's Telegram channel. In that call or video, dreams and money are displayed and stock market technicalities are thrown at you with jargon.

In the Telegram channel, you see this amazing announcement:

> **Account Management Service**
>
> - *Available at profit sharing of 50–50 only*
> - Get best profit on your account without any risk.
> - Minimum deposit: ₹50,000

- All brokers accepted
- Sure-shot trade
- 50–50 profit-sharing basis
- Maximum risk of 5 per cent only
- 20 per cent to 30 per cent profit on daily basis
- Daily profit sharing

Kindly share the following details:

- Login ID
- Password
- Pin
- Broker
- Mobile number

Seems lucrative enough. And for some, it may be. This is followed by a call to action that says, 'If you want this service, just CALL or MESSAGE us on this number.'

Let's say this Telegram message is seen by about 1,000 people or this video is watched by 10,000 people every time. How many of them will be urged to perform that 'call to action'. There will always be a few. Across countries, across generations.

Let's say one such person makes a call. Here is how that would go:

Scammer: 'Hello!'

Victim: 'Hi, yes. This is Faizan. Is this Market Marvels? I saw your message in the Telegram channel. I have been following you for the tips and levels you have been providing. I also see a lot of profit screenshots every day on that channel.'

Scammer: 'Yes, sure. How can I help you?'

Victim: 'I… I want to make money from the stock market but I don't know much. Can you help somehow?'

Scammer: 'Of course. I can manage your demat account and you don't even have to pay me a fee for that.'

Victim: 'What, really? It's free?'

Scammer: 'There is no fee. With my 10-plus years of experience in stock market trading, I will handle your account. You put in the capital, I trade, I make profit and take a cut of the profit. You don't have to do anything.'

Victim: 'Okay. But what if there is a loss?'

Scammer: 'There is never a loss when I trade.'

Victim: 'But this is the stock market, right? Losses can happen. It happened to me last year.'

Scammer: 'Sure, but I cut my losses early. I put in a proper stop-loss, and let's say there is a loss, in which case I make sure to get the recovery done in the next trade. I manage hundreds of accounts in parallel. It's your choice. You can let me know.'

Victim: 'Sure. I would like to start but I will start small. I will fund my account with ₹50,000 and then we will see.'

The fund value may vary but most stories start more or less like this and end pretty much the same way too. Let's understand what happens in the first few days.

If there was an initial profit:

Victim: 'Hey, Market Marvels. Thank you! We made money yesterday. You are a genius.'

Scammer: 'Yes—₹20,000 profit on ₹50,000. That's just okay money.'

Ting!

Victim: 'I just transferred ₹10,000 to your account. I am also putting in ₹4 lakh more Let's keep going.'

Scammer: 'Hmmm...'

The good days go on for some time, and then follows the climax, which is always a cliche.

Victim: 'Hey, my account is blown completely. You lost ₹4.5 lakh yesterday. I kept calling to tell you to not make any further trades but you did not even answer or read any of my messages.'

Scammer: 'It's the stock market, this happens. Don't worry. Just fund your account with another ₹5 lakh and I will get us back on the road.'

Victim: 'But this is what I had. I don't have any more money.'

Scammer: 'Get it from a friend or ask a relative. Take a loan. If you want to recover, funds are required. I can't trade without money.'

Victim: 'You told me you never lose.'

Scammer: 'Fund the account!'

Victim: 'But...'

Call disconnected.

From here, the story ends in two ways. One is painful; the other is painful but with much more dire consequences. Most the people put an end to the story here. They regret their actions, move on, abuse the stock market, and forget about everything.

But a few ask for money from whomsoever they can. They lost money already, but are now on their way to lose their social status, credibility, trust, and in some extreme cases even their dignity.

Why?

They want to recover their money. They think they HAVE to. They seem to have lost their way. They don't think straight. More funds are put in, more calls to people such as Market Marvels are made. There are more regrets in the making.

I have heard people saying:

I put in the money that my father gave me for my college fee.
I stole my mother's jewellery and sold it for cash.
I put my father's grocery shop as collateral for a bank loan.

There is no number to quote but there are also some stories that end in suicides—from techies[3] [4] and families[5] to the unemployed[6].

The worst part is that most of these deaths are silent. No one knows what really happened. Often, even the families have no answers.

What is to be learnt here?

No one is making videos and sending messages showcasing their skills in stock market trading and professing their intention to make a lot of money for your benefit. If they had these skills, they would use their own money.

If the person is short of money, they can take loans in their own name since they are so confident of the skills they have for stock market trading. Why would they need someone else's demat account or someone else's money to trade and make

---

[3]TNN, 'Techie Jumps to Death after Losses in Share Market', *The Times of India*, 12 November 2023, https://tinyurl.com/aebh38v. Accessed on 3 March 2025.

[4]Singh, Shubham, 'Stung by Stock Market Losses, Andhra Techie Commits Suicide after Killing Wife, Two Daughters, Says Report', *Business Today*, 5 August 2023, https://tinyurl.com/bdctru65. Accessed on 3 March 2025.

[5]'"Stock Market Losses" Drive Son, Mom to Death in Kolkata', *The Telegraph Online*, 20 February 2022, https://tinyurl.com/yzm64xds. Accessed on 3 March 2025.

[6]Kshitiz, 'Unemployed Man Dies by Suicide After Incurring Losses in the Stock Market', *The Times of India*, 25 December 2024, https://tinyurl.com/bddcdm8y. Accessed on 3 March 2025.

money? Why would they live with 40 per cent or 50 per cent profit? Why wouldn't they want to take home 100 per cent of the profits?

There is only one reason for this.

They don't have that skill. They don't understand risk management. They don't have the psychology to trade with large capital. They just log in from different demat accounts to play this game. Sometimes they win, sometimes they lose. They don't owe anything to anyone and there is no responsibility to take care of.

But you must be responsible with your own money. You have worked hard for it.

How can you just give away all that money to someone because you think they can make you more money?

There is only one person who can make you more money: YOU.

If you really want to make more money from stock market trading, learn it. Do not trust anyone sending gimmicks like this. There is no doubt that you can make money from the stock market. These are real companies working day and night for their own profits. There is a high chance that at least some will see their share prices going up over a period of time.

The videos or reels or Telegram messages mentioned above are enough for you to understand that these are scams—20 to 30 per cent profit per day, a maximum risk of 5 per cent, sure-shot trades. Don't you see these are nothing but enticements? If you get persuaded, it only exposes your greed. Hide it. Bury that emotion somewhere for your own greater good.

Once you get scammed and reach out to the regulator, there is a high chance that you will not get help. The simple reason is that the person who scammed you has nothing to do with NSE or SEBI and is just trapping people. The best you can do is to file an FIR in a local police station and file a court case.

As far as the NSE is concerned, at best they will send out an advisory to all the retail investors and market infrastructure institutions with the details of the scamster. There will be a disclaimer in the advisory that the regulator and exchanges have nothing to do with this scamster.

Here is a quick look at one such advisory for your reference:

> Dear Customers,
>
> Greetings of the day!
> In our continuous effort to keep you safeguarded from market-related frauds and to increase awareness while conducting trades, we request you to ensure that you do not engage with the individual mentioned below:
>
> - Person named Manish Sharma (name changed) operating through mobile number 777xxxx141 is providing tips and calls for trading and making profit-sharing arrangements.
> - Investors are cautioned and advised not to subscribe to any such scheme/product offered by any person/entity offering indicative/assured/guaranteed returns in the stock market as the same is prohibited by law. Participation in such prohibited schemes/platforms is at investors' own risk, cost and consequences. Further, investors are advised not to share their trading credentials such as user ID/password/OTP/PIN with anyone. Accordingly, we request you to be cautious and ensure that you do not engage in any activities with such persons/entities.

So manage your expectations accordingly.

What happens when you become a fan of someone or something? You don't even realize that in your love for the person or entity, you could end up being made a scapegoat. The other person might be using their fame to misguide you financially.

Who are these finfluencers?

But before we talk about social media finfluencers, we need to talk about their predecessors—the OG finfluencers.

Part 3

FINFLUENCER SCAMS

7

THE ORIGINAL FINFLUENCERS

'*Arey* Dadu, why do you keep watching these business TV channels every morning?' I remember asking my grandfather this during my engineering days, back in 2002–03.

'Shh...you won't understand, *beta*. Let's talk once you are back from college,' he used to say while glued to the TV. This was one of his ways to avoid having a longer conversation with anyone when the market was trading.

He used to be very focused and listened to what TV hosts and guests had to say about generic market and company news, what was going on, and then analysed what might happen. Overall, he made a decent return on his investments over the years while losing a little. He told me one day: 'I watch, I analyse, and if I like what I see, I invest.' He also cautioned me about what we were being fed across various media.

Before proceeding further, go through these cases:

Case 1

An amount of ₹29,518,680 to be impounded from Mr Hemant Ghai for front-running under PFUTP (Prohibition of Fraudulent & Unfair Trading Practices) through his TV shows *Stock 20-20*, *Munafe Ki Taiyari Pehla Sauda* and *Kamai Ka Adda*.

He is also restrained from buying, selling or dealing in securities, either directly or indirectly, in any manner whatsoever till further directions.

The bank accounts of Mr Hemant Ghai, Ms Jaya Hemant Ghai (wife) and Ms Shyam Mohini Ghai (mother) are frozen for debit till further directions/ communications.[7]

Case 2

SEBI barred Pradeep Pandya, who was anchoring the stock market show *Pandya Ka Funda* on CNBC Awaaz. He also hosted/co-hosted shows such as *Pehla Sauda* (8:55 a.m. on weekdays), *Aakhri Sauda* (1:55 p.m. on weekdays), *10 Ke Dumdaar Trade* (9:57 a.m.).

He must return ₹65,221,703.37 jointly and severally along with 2 others.[8]

Case 3

SEBI has slapped a fine of ₹7.41 crore against 5 entities who were part of the guest panel of the Zee Business news channel.

Kiran Jadhav, Ashish Kelkar, Himanshu Gupta, Mudit Goyal, and Simi Bhaumik have been referred to as 'Guest Experts', who have allegedly provided non-public information to the profit makers before the broadcasting of their recommendations.[9]

---

[7]'Order in the Matter of CNBC Awaaz Shows Co-Hosted by Mr. Hemant Ghai', Securities and Exchange Board of India (SEBI), 22 July 2022, https://tinyurl.com/tzkdxnr8. Accessed on 3 March 2025.

[8]'Interim Order in the Matter of Alpesh Furiya and Connected Entities Trading Ahead of Recommendations of Mr. Pradeep Pandya, Anchor on Shows of CNBC Awaaz', Securities and Exchange Board of India (SEBI), 4 October 2021, https://tinyurl.com/mpwf6s2r. Accessed on 3 March 2025.

[9]'Settlement Order in the Matter of Trading Based on the Stock Recommendations Given by Guest Experts Appearing on Zee Business

What are these cases? Who are these people? Why were they penalized?

The context here revolves around business TV channels that run stock market-related news and shows through the day. There are hosts, guests and financial experts who appear on various shows, giving financial advice, recommendations or market commentary. Most of these shows are genuine but in a few cases everything is done to manipulate the viewers. The above cases and the penalties discussed are real.

But why are we discussing these cases?

Apart from social media conversations, we must remember that TV and digital/print media are also sources of stock market information and education. In fact, TV and print media were the original finfluencers, or financial influencers.

Social media is very recent, while we have all grown up with newspapers and magazines in one hand and the TV remote in the other. All of us have consumed hours of TV content and read thousands of lines of news in the daily papers.

Now imagine this.

What if those who have been reading or watching financial content all their lives learn that there might have been instances where they were misinformed about something? And that this was done so that the host, production house, TV channel, newspaper company and so on wanted to benefit from your actions based on that piece of information.

What if the news headline you read today recommending you buy a stock was the one that the editor had already stocked upon? What if the listed company paid the host to say good things about the stock on the show you watch on a business channel?

Channel', Securities and Exchange Board of India (SEBI), 16 January 2025, https://tinyurl.com/mr23atfp. Accessed on 3 March 2025.

What if the guest expert is just a paid dummy from a penny stock company who is there to pump up the stock by recommending it to the audience and then dump it at a higher price?

These are not just hypotheticals.

These are the stories mentioned earlier where even SEBI passed penalty orders against such entities.

The famous business channel CNBC Awaaz had Hemant Ghai as its host for a show called *Stock 20-20*, which aired on weekdays at 7:20 a.m. On this show, which had a sizeable audience, Ghai used to recommend stocks for the day. This happened every day during the week and obviously a chunk of the audience used to place trades in the recommended stocks.

The twist was that Ghai placed trades in those very stocks before he recommended them and then the viewers watching the show would take a position in those same stocks. It was a hit show that people loved.

The main thing to understand here is that when a sizeable number of people take a position in a particular stock, the price generally goes up at least momentarily. This happened in the stocks that Ghai recommended. Since he already held positions in those stocks, once the price would see a marginal or decent increase, he would exit those stocks and pocket the profits.

To circumvent the law, he used his wife's and mother's demat accounts to place these mischievous trades. He made a whopping ₹2.95 crore in this manner. In regulatory terms, this is called front-running fraud under PFUTP, SEBI Regulations 2003.[10]

---

[10]Front-running is an illegal practice under SEBI Act, 1992, and PFUTP (Prohibition of Fraudulent & Unfair Trading Practices) where an advisor, trader, broker or anyone with an influence places a trade on a specific security first and then passes on the same trade as a market recommendation to his or her audience or user base. By doing so, he or she takes an unfair advantage to make a potential profit on that trade.

SEBI may be slow in its proceedings but when a case is picked up, it reaches an end.

The case of Hemant Ghai also ended but not in the way he would have preferred. He thought he was smart enough to get away and so he never saw it coming. He was penalized ₹3.9 crore as ill-gotten gains from his activities. Ghai, his wife and mother were barred from the capital markets for indulging in fraudulent trading practices.

Fraud on the Inside, Genuine on the Outside

No fraudster is the same and some can even pass off as genuine and authentic. How? Paid PR, that's how. Have a look at these names. Md. Nasir[11], PR Sundar[12] [13], Asmita Patel[14]. What is common among all of them? They all have had editorials written about them by prominent media houses. They have also been caught red-handed by SEBI and penalized heavily.

At any given point, SEBI is investigating finfluencers violating major prohibitions (such as assured returns, offering tips and advisory without relevant licence). In the recent past,

---

[11]'MD Nasir, the Trading Educator, Passes A Few Pieces of Advice for the Budding Traders', *Latestly*, 4 July 2022, https://tinyurl.com/ycb5sz4a. Accessed on 3 March 2025.

[12]Asthana, Shishir, 'From a Maths Teacher to India's Leading Option Seller: The Inspiring Journey of PR Sundar', *Moneycontrol*, 12 August 2018, https://tinyurl.com/ycx6c7jh. Accessed on 3 March 2025.

[13]Kriplani, Jash, 'Trading Income Is One Part of My Business: PR Sundar', *Mint*, 18 November 2022, https://tinyurl.com/mr2k2abz. Accessed on 3 March 2025.

[14]ET Bureau, 'Market Mastermind Asmita Patel Says Day Trading Is Injurious to Wealth, Suggests Only 15 Minutes of Screen Time', *The Economic Times*, 2 August 2022, https://tinyurl.com/mr32u8za. Accessed on 3 March 2025.

finfluencers such as PR Sundar[15], Md. Nasir[16], Asmita Patel[17], Ravindra Bharti[18] and Bishal Phukan[19] have been penalized.

These social media influencers were everywhere, promoting luxury and premium lifestyles while highlighting their 'course' or 'subscription' as the magic source. This was nothing but an open heist happening right in front of the stock market regulator.

So SEBI had to do something.

While there were hundreds or maybe thousands of such fake finfluencers violating all sorts of rules and regulations, SEBI had to set some examples. These were to set the record straight, which they did to an extent.

For instance, while PR Sundar was offering investment advice without any SEBI licence, Md. Nasir was shouting 'guaranteed returns' at the top of his voice. Asmita Patel packaged her unregistered advisories with courses that cost ₹7 lakh. Nishan Singh from Sanbun Investments handled his clients' trading

---

[15] 'Settlement Order in Respect of Mansun Consultancy Private Limited, Mr. P.R. Sundar, and Ms. Mangayarkarasi Sundar', Securities and Exchange Board of India, 25 May 2023, https://tinyurl.com/979xj92s. Accessed on 3 March 2025.

[16] 'Final Order in the Matter of Unregistered Investment Advisory Activities by Baap of Chart', Securities and Exchange Board of India, 2 December 2024, https://tinyurl.com/y2hjsutz. Accessed on 3 March 2025.

[17] 'Order in the Matter of Asmita Patel Global School of Trading Private Limited', Securities and Exchange Board of India, 7 February 2025, https://tinyurl.com/4strkhmu. Accessed on 3 March 2025.

[18] 'Order in the Matter of Ravindra Bharti Education Institute Private Limited', Securities and Exchange Board of India, 5 April 2024, https://tinyurl.com/yyszw4au. Accessed on 3 March 2025.

[19] 'CBI Files Chargesheet Against Four Accused in Dibrugarh Investment Scam Case (One of the 41 Assam Investment Scam Cases) Before the Special CBI Court, Guwahati', Central Bureau of Investigation, 28 November 2024, https://tinyurl.com/f8zpt4e5. Accessed on 3 March 2025.

accounts without any licensing.

It needs to be understood that all news websites, papers, magazines and channels get paid for sponsored pieces. However, some of them fail to do the single most important thing—due diligence of the person/entity being promoted.

As in the case of a YouTube channel hosting podcasts, it is unethical to invite guests without doing background checks—or in the case of a social media influencer, to promote a product without validating its authenticity and legality. In the same way, it becomes even more important for the OG finfluencers to follow suit, if not lead the way.

TV and print media have had their share of similar concerns when it comes to retail traders. Obviously, not all TV channels, newspapers or magazines performed such gimmicks, and similarly, not everybody on social media is a fraudster. Only those finfluencers who place greed over ethics are poison in the social media space. Every platform, TV channel, newspaper, radio channel, magazine or social media finfluencer that has reach and distribution has a responsibility not to play with the trust of their audience. Public interest must come first.

As for the public, we need to learn not to react immediately to everything we see or read. Take a deep breath, or maybe two, and follow the advice my grandfather used to give, which we discussed at the start of this chapter. I do, to this day.

However, it is a natural impulse to follow someone on YouTube, Instagram or any other platform. The million-dollar question then is: How do you know that the influencer you are following is genuine or fake? Do they mean well or are there hidden intentions?

8

ARE YOU FOLLOWING A GENUINE FINFLUENCER?

'And this is what an IPO is!'

'Options are basically contracts where two parties are involved…'

'This is my chart analysis and this stock seems bullish to me. Having said that, make sure to perform your own analysis or check with your financial advisor before investing.'

Modest Beginnings: Covid and Boredom

There was a short period of time where there were very few finance channels on social media, primarily YouTube. I am talking about 2016–17 and maybe even some part of 2018. I know this because our first video was published in January 2017.

Our initial videos talked about the structure of the stock market, the role of the regulator, stockbrokers, exchanges, and how the whole ecosystem works. This was 2017 and people were just getting warmed up to the internet and information in a video format. These informational videos were a niche for people who took the stock market seriously.

Then a few channels were launched where stock levels were a point of almost everyday discussion. Maybe they did not know that this was not in line with SEBI regulations. Having said that, there was no real clarity either.

Time passed. Covid kicked in. People started staying at home. The supply of consumers (read viewers) for financial content increased manifold. All industries were shut except the stock market. People had savings and a decent chunk of the workforce was getting salaries. People at home were also bored.

With the stock market being the only active thing around and a lot of financial influencers talking about stocks regularly, suddenly everybody in the country wanted to be a trader or an investor, but mostly the former. People had two options:

1. Learn slowly and gradually to become a trader or investor.
2. Follow a few channels where stocks were being discussed and ask specific stocks-related questions.

Most people decided to choose Option 2.

This was because it seemed to be a quicker way to make money. Of course, that statement turned out to be 50 per cent correct. It was a quicker way—but to lose money. When the demand for such a second option started rising, so did its supply. The quality of financial education content providers did not increase at the same pace, but the supply of opportunists did.

This new wave of financial influencers had some fake ones thrown in. They were not actually financial influencers but they saw an opportunity to become one as people wanted such content. We call them 'fake-finfluencers'. In fact, we run a series on our channel 'A Digital Blogger' with the same title.

Fake influencers had an audience now and they also had a mission—to make a lot of money. The audience base was ready to shell out ₹5,000–₹10,000 a month to anyone who convinced them they knew what they were doing. They even paid ₹50,000 if someone had a stronger social media footprint. If any fake finfluencer had good sales skills, a lot of these viewers were ready to add another zero to this amount.

Who or What Is a Fake-Finfluencer?

A finfluencer is someone who wants to create or has created a reputation in a niche financially focused audience, be it stock market investments, trading, mutual funds, insurance, personal finance or anything else related to money.

This definition also has a broader definition that goes beyond YouTubers and Instagram influencers. For instance, finance news websites, blogs, print media, financial newspapers/magazines, finance TV channels and personalities on those channels can all be seen as finfluencers.

I would even say if a known personality from a different stream of work—viz. a movie star, a cricketer or a politician—talks about a specific stock or the market in general, they would also be a finfluencer.

How?

Simple. There is no official certification to be a finfluencer or for any kind of influencer. So, if someone creates a following based on financial content or someone has a general following and gives them financial advice, either way both are influencing their audience on finances.

Having said all this, I will admit that a lot of finfluencers are genuine. These are the people who are trying to teach you personal finance, telling you stock market investments, talking about hard-core financial concepts in a simple language, and trying to tell you about the industry and regulations.

Fake Finfluencers' Rise

While a major chunk of the trading audience had left the stock market after Covid passed, fake finfluencers still stuck around. The traders had decided to term trading as 'gambling' because they had not just lost the fee amount that they had paid to finfluencers but a lot more. This extra money was what they had put into the market based on the recommendations or strategies they had gotten for the money they had paid.

However, there was something else brewing because the audience of these fake finfluencers was still stable even as they were leaving the stock market. How?

The scale of their reach did not change. People did. While one left calling the stock market a casino, two new ones who wanted to get rich came in. In India, the number of active demat accounts saw an increase from 10,795,660 to 18,893,832 in a single year from 2019 to 2020.[20] A jump of 42.3 per cent—something the Indian stock market had never seen from a numeral increase point of view.

Furthermore, the barrier of entry for new traders got lower thanks to SEBI's intraday margin rule that pushed a decent chunk of traders into something called options trading. This had a huge role to play in what was going to happen next.

People started getting into derivatives or options trading since that's what attracted newer traders. You could be an option trader with just ₹1,000 or ₹2,000 in your pocket. A lot of college-going students and individuals with new jobs had access to that

[20]'Report 1C: Redressal of Complaints Lodged by Clients Against Trading Members (TMs) during 2024–25', last updated on 31 January 2025, National Stock Exchange of India, https://tinyurl.com/2kyh2rnu. Accessed on 3 March 2025.

kind of money. And those with a stable salary could obviously also spare that money.

A decent percentage of this new stock market population started expecting their capital to double by the end of the day. This was the perception built around this format of trading. Quite a few fake YouTube influencers were encouraging this idea in their Telegram channels.

The social media footprint of such influencers had also widened to Instagram—and Instagram demanded strong visuals. These fake finfluencers opted to show riches, money and glamour from success stories even if they had to fake it (most of them actually did). If you could show cash in and around your computer, car, mobile phone, anywhere, it would help build credibility. These fake finfluencers created an environment where they assumed their audience was expecting them to have made it big from the stock market.

One after another, this turned out to be a long train, building peer pressure. If you had to build these audiences, you had to have money and you had to show it off.

What is the ground situation today?

Here's our example.

As part of content creation for our YouTube channel 'A Digital Blogger', we investigate many cases of people being scammed by finfluencers. In our videos, there is a form pinned in the description that viewers can fill in and explain what they went through. We call such victims and try to understand their concerns. Then, to validate the accusations levied, we become a client of that finfluencer and gain practical experience.

Let's take one such case.

The person's name is Anil (name changed). If you check some of his reels, you will find:

- A display of PnL statements always showing a profit
- Persuasion to join his Telegram channel/online course/offline classes
- An assurance to make everyone a profitable trader
- A push to the audience to leave their full-time jobs and join his services

Basically, this person lures his audience into the stock market and then pitches his paid services. A few users mentioned this person to us.

It's relatively easy to investigate and research apps, Telegram or WhatsApp groups, as well as live sessions. The thing with 'Trade with Anil' was that he was offering his 'classes' offline. There was an online app but that wouldn't have shown us the complete picture. This offline batch was for one month in a city which was 350 km away from us.

Well, I believe that when you ask for things from the universe, it has a way to granting them. It was a Friday evening and we were having an internal team meeting about app marketing when some of us started discussing the Anil case during a break. Suddenly, one of our team members, Vedansh (name changed), stood up and said 'I will go.'

I was really surprised.

'Are you sure? And how will you even manage? You will have to live there for a month amongst people you don't know and also investigate the case.'

'Yes, sir. I have been thinking about it for a while. But I am sure that I would like to check out this case,' Vedansh said confidently.

We looked at each other and then said, 'Yes!'

The agenda of the meeting changed to Vedansh's plan of action for this case.

He stayed there for a month and found out it was all just a mockery of students who had come from different parts of the country persuaded by the Instagram reels. It was not even a month but just 24 days. In all that time, the fake finfluencer only took five classes himself. There was a hostel which was just a huge single room with 15–20 beds all tucked together, with everyone sharing one washroom; there were 3–4 such hostels.

Each student had to pay a fee of ₹18,000 and if someone wanted to stay in a hostel, there was an additional charge of ₹10,000. It was all a hoax. No lives were changed and people went back to their previous lives, forgetting the experience.

In our online research, we found that Anil was selling tips and recommendations in equity and options trading. There were hundreds of screenshots with unsolicited stock market tips—without any SEBI licence—in his free Telegram channel. He also regularly promoted 'dabba trading', a banned format in India.

Dabba trading is an illegal parallel to the stock market where orders are marked but not executed in any of the exchanges. These transactions happen in cash.

Basically, there was a lot of fancy and fake stuff going on. And all of that was happening by inducing and luring people into the stock market. Those people were not supposed to be there in the first place; they never wanted to be there.

This is one of the biggest traits of a fake finfluencer. They show unrealistic possibilities and paint a picture of a world that is like a dream come true for any lower- or middle-class person who want to make it big. Eventually the bubble bursts for anyone who pays. Some fortunately use others' experiences to get out of the dream world on their own.

So, after all this, how does one identify a fake finfluencer from an honest one?

Honestly, with all the shadiness in this space, it's surprisingly easy to filter out the genuine ones who shine like diamonds in dirt. Honest finfluencers not only educate but also make people aware of the dangers, loopholes, gaps and threats of investing in stock market. They do not suggest anything that they have not personally validated, verified, consumed and checked. They offer a realistic picture, not fancy dreams. The biggest green flag is that these finfluencers only share tips or recommendations if they are a SEBI-registered advisor or analyst. They always warn the viewer about the potential hazards related to their strategy and in most cases will not charm you with an extravagant lifestyle.

While even these people make mistakes, it's easy to tell the difference between a mistake and an intentional gimmick. The best finfluencers in this space apologize, accept the mistake, and if possible, correct it.

To judge someone online, you must first remove the fan/hater cap. Nobody should be a hero and nobody should be a villain. You need to be objective and look at the full story to understand the complete context. Do some real research and then take a call.

It seems tedious to find a genuine financial content creator but there are still many out there. Always remember that even after you have done your research, never put the person on a pedestal and all validation must be regular. As long as you are trying to follow and learn from the person, your trust must have a price tag. Remember, influencers in any field are there to motivate you, but don't try to copy their lives.

9

HOW TO IDENTIFY A FAKE FINFLUENCER?

There are fakes of everything, everything that is worthy. Worthy enough to be faked. There is fake gold, fake shoes, fake food, fake people. Similarly, there is something called a fake-finfluencer.

Once I came across a YouTube channel where I saw the finfluencer walking out of a luxury Mercedes car, getting down to a five-star hotel, and then swaying along with bodyguards towards a well-lit stage. Full swag!

Now, there is nothing wrong with showing off stuff. It's a personal choice. The problem is when the same person goes ahead and makes statements like: 'Whatever I am teaching, make sure you use that every day in your trades. You will get profits GUARANTEED.'

Any rational person would know that all these things are not possible in the stock market. Only the gullible or greedy could fall in those traps. We call them sheep. Identifying such a person is honestly very easy. All you have to do is think objectively.

We've talked about who are fake-finfluencers. Now, you may think, how can someone be a fake-finfluencer?

In the world of social media, influencers are the stars who people believe and follow for specific advice and in general too. They can be seen as SMEs or subject-matter experts of any kind within their industry domain. You would find travel influencers, health and fitness ones, movie experts. You get the point. But there would be a few in any of the niches who would be milking their audience by showing things that are just wrong, technically or ethically. The audience trusts them and the stuff they say or show. After all, they are the followers. Therefore, they follow their influencer stars even when the product or service they are marketing is ingenuine.

And what exactly is ingenuine? Anything that is not in the interest of the follower.

Let's go deeper.

In finance space, anyone who does the following can be seen as a fake-finfluencer:

- Sharing trading tips with RA licence via WhatsApp, Telegram channels, etc.
- Recommending unregulated products such as binary, forex trading, etc.
- Suggesting gambling platforms through paid promotions or organically.
- Someone who is a loss-making trading entity but is claiming to be otherwise.
- Using clone trading apps.
- Offering assured-returns strategy or anything that has zero-loss outcome.
- Profit-sharing scheme providers.

Basically, if you detach yourself emotionally and keep your greed away while learning something online, you will get to know who is real and who is not.

But why are they doing so? Simple: money or fame. Or both.

There are a lot of brands who would pay them to say stuff that they should not ideally be saying. Promoting betting apps or unregulated financial products, or recommending stocks as they are being paid by the listed company itself, is not just ethically but a lot of times also legally wrong. Sometimes, you will find someone recommending that you invest in an IPO. You may never know that the person has been paid by a third-party marketing agency, who in turn has been paid by the IPO company, to say that. Then, there are finfluencers who would just say extreme stuff so that you can buy their personal product or service.

Fake-Finfluencer Types

First, ideally you must not be getting influenced by anyone out there when it comes to your finances. When you go online and follow such influencers, you can keep expectations to the levels of learning or becoming aware online, at best. However, doing stuff such as buying and selling stocks, mutual funds, insurance or taking research advisory on the basis that your favourite YouTuber or Instagrammer has said so, makes ZERO sense. Novices end up believing that everything that they see on social media is true and honest.

Second, there are people who are greedy enough to really wish that what they are seeing is, hopefully, true and somehow their life can also see a turnaround.

Do you fall into any of these categories?

Here are some quick ways for you to identify these foxes.

The first and foremost attribute of a fake-finfluencer is that he/she is busy seeing dreams for others. You don't need to study; you don't need to work under someone. You can be your own boss; stock market will help you do all of that. These dreams are shown to everyone without understanding their context or situation in life. That is, the same dream is now being seen by a 12th-pass student who is focused on taking the IIT exam and someone working in an IT company, doing well for the last three-four years.

Their life priorities will, temporarily, change for now. They would want all of that shown in that reel because a fake-finfluencer showed them that unrealistic dream. We need to understand one thing here. Making money by trading in the stock market is not just about skill. It depends on your capital amount for sure, but it is also about your needs, your limits, your main/alternate sources of income, your opportunity cost, your family condition, your personality, and so on.

How can someone over a YouTube or Instagram video tell you that you can be rich and famous and make shit-loads of money by following their strategy? Wouldn't you want to use your head before changing your current commitments in life?

Shows you money and riches

Let me ask you something. Have you ever met a poor- or mediocre-looking real-estate agent? Most likely you have not. Does that mean there are no poor real-estate agents? Of course, there are.

I have a few friends in real-estate across cities and one fine day, I asked this question to one of those friends, Sanchit: 'How do you afford the riches?'

'We can't. Still we have to,' he said.

'What do you mean you HAVE to?' my curiosity increased.

'It's not that difficult to understand, Aseem. The properties we sell are worth crores of rupees and for customers who visit real-estate agents like me, we cannot have a mediocre office.

'If we sit in an office as per our actual budgets, those richie-rich people won't place their trust in us. They would wonder if such a person can pull off a five-crore deal.'

'Does every real-estate agent do this?' I was intrigued.

'Of course not. It's not that every real-estate agent does this but it's an unwritten rule some of us follow,' he answered, taking a sip from his gold-plated tea cup.

The fake-finfluencers are no different. A few choose to show you things they don't even own—or maybe they do, claiming that they got all of that with the money from stock market, although that isn't always the case.

Guaranteeing profit

Remember, when someone says guarantee of one per cent profit, the problem is not with the one per cent but with the word 'guarantee'. A said-guarantee of even one per cent is illegal and unrealistic. It's illegal because this goes against the SEBI rules and regulations where no one is allowed to use such terms. And it's unrealistic for the simple reason that it is the stock market and every investment here is subject to market risk. So, there is no guarantee of anything here. Thus, if someone gives you that, it's a direct signal for you to run in the opposite direction.

In fact, even a SEBI-registered IA or RA can't use those terms, and here we are talking about an unregistered fake-finfluencer. This chapter, I think, should be enough for you to understand the difference between a genuine finfluencer and a fake one.

So, make your online choices on social media based on such objectivity.

10

WHAT A YOUTUBER CAN LEGALLY SAY IN VIDEOS

Is there a way to know whether what your favourite YouTuber is saying in their videos is legal or not? Is there is a possibility that the person might be saying something, knowingly or unknowingly, that is against the rules of the regulator?

The answer is yes.

So let's dive into the SEBI rulebook.

'Aseem, remember one thing. The devil is always in the details,' Gagan Singla, my boss at Angel One, used to tell me. This was when I was working as Vice President, Digital, at Angel One, one of India's leading stockbrokers.

In line with this advice, the current chapter delves into all the things that can be done in the financial space that are completely above board. This chapter talks to the audience, the viewers and the followers of finfluencers who are serious about learning about finance, investments and the stock market. It also focuses on the finfluencers of today and the future, about what they can talk about in their videos, posts or any other format of content they post.

Here's a discussion I had recently.

It was 7 January 2024, a Sunday. I was playing with my kids at home.

My phone rang. It was someone I knew, a YouTube influencer

from the finance community with a subscriber base of more than two million. I had recently met him in an event where we exchanged numbers.

'Hey, how are you, Aseem?' he said.

'I am good, how have you been?'

'Good too. I needed some quick advice from you. I have been watching your videos about regulations,' he said.

'Sure man, tell me,' I responded.

'Okay, so I put out a lot of content around IPOs. I do my primary research based on the documents submitted by the company, then do some competitive analysis, and so on. The content is my own research with no biases. Yes, I do have some sponsored content, but then I always mention that in the video. Is that okay? Am I doing anything wrong that can hurt me later?' he continued.

'I don't think so,' I replied. 'Tell me something honestly. Are you in contact with the promoters or the directors of the company who are looking to get listed?'

'No, of course not. I don't even conduct any interviews of the founders or directors of such companies before they go public,' he answered.

'There is nothing wrong in interviewing them, but there must not be any background marketing activity going on, for which you get paid by them and you claim the video to be 100 per cent organic,' I explained.

'Sure, got it. I have not gone into that lane,' he said.

'Super. You are solid then,' I said, ending the call.

We then went on with our respective Sundays.

I bring this up to highlight that there are creators who want to do the right thing. This was one of the many conversations I have been having due to the kind of content we push.

The Thick Line

We also get a lot of questions from traders about the content in someone's YouTube channel. Viewers ask us whether what was being said by the finfluencer was in line with regulations. Now, with the information we are aware of, there is a thick line on what can be said and what can't be. But there are also exceptions within the written rules.

Here are just a few things a finance-based YouTuber can say that add value for the user:

- Educational content
- Awareness
- General information
- Book reviews
- Financial news
- Current micro- and macro-level commentary on events

These influencers still get confused when it comes to figuring out what exactly are they allowed to say within SEBI regulations. Some questions we get are whether they can say:

- According to me, Tech Mahindra stock has a good chance to make a return of 15 per cent in the next 2 months.
- I think the Nifty will touch 23,000 by the end of this month.
- Guys, I am going to place a trade in Tata Motors stock at a price of ₹1,100 and may exit at ₹1,000 or ₹1,300 based on my risk-reward.

In general plain language:

- You can talk about investment and trading products in general.

- You can talk about stock analysis.
- You can even talk about the past performance of stock using a chart analysis.

But talk of future performance or percentage/numeral value-based expected movements and levels—both high and low and anything that is directional or concrete with numbers—can be seen as a tip, recommendation or something close to that.

You could be asked why you named that particular stock at that particular level.

You may say it was your analysis. That you never took money from any viewer or user for telling them about that stock. That your bank account can be checked. However, there are too many things that can happen in the background.

For instance, there could be situations where it is not a B2C (business to consumer or user) setup but a B2B (business to business or company) one. This implies that one may not have taken any cash or consideration from the person with whom the tip was shared but there could have been something between the influencer and the business whose stock was being discussed.

Imagine 100,000 people taking a position on this stock just because a famous YouTuber said so. Or maybe the advice was given on a Telegram channel that has a subscriber base of 500,000. Think of what could happen when so many people follow this advice and take a position in the stock. It will trade in huge volumes, kicking its price higher. The influencer will also see a huge jump in their bank account. This deal can be done in cash or in the form of a gift.

Here's an anecdote:

'You can't even imagine how payments are made for stock manipulation,' a well-known finfluencer told me.

'There are people in the community who subtly give a stock

recommendation through their videos and do not charge money from the listed companies,' he continued.

'What do you mean? I am pretty sure they don't do it for free,' I responded.

'Paintings,' he said.

'Art-loving traders?' I was still confused.

'*Arey* Aseem Babu, these paintings are not normal pieces. They have a huge ask in the black market where they are sold for crores.'

I was not expecting that.

Influencers can also make money in the wrong way through something called front-running.

What if a YouTuber has already taken a position in a stock? A position with his complete net worth. He goes live at 9.15 a.m. He recommends the stock and says, 'You know what, I love this stock and where this is going.' Now, he waits for the magic to happen. The YouTuber now sees the same magic within his reach that the promoter saw in their valuation in the first case. He cuts the position at 9.25 a.m. and his net worth is already 1.1X of the value it was 10 minutes back. That's 10 per cent profit in 10 minutes. That's how powerful this can be.

Having said this, SEBI has not reached this depth of scrutiny yet. It is still at the point where it is reacting to complaints made by users on direct tips. There are suo moto cases where the regulator taps into something fishy but this happens very rarely. This is a major reason why such fake-finfluencers are so overconfident.

The Takeaway

If you are somebody who wants to do honest work by creating stock market content, keep yourself clean by creating content that is within ethics and regulations. At the same time, if you are someone who watches a lot of financial content, keep an eye out for people who do all the fancy stuff I've mentioned and avoid them. Their real interests are hidden.

Let's reiterate what a YouTuber or an influencer can say in the financial space:

- Analysing charts is okay.
- Back-testing is okay.
- Showing a strategy is also okay in a setup with its risk-reward.
- Sharing information on company fundamentals, its promoters, and comparison with its peers is also okay. IPO discussion can be seen as healthy too.
- Option-chain analysis.
- Indicators and their usage.

The point is you can talk about concepts, strategies, analysis, trading products and asset classes in general. The more specific you get, the more concerning it becomes. Ideally do not be specific about price levels: i.e., target price, stop-loss, your entry/exit prices, and so on.

The same applies for YouTube Live. However, the risks associated with that format of content are at a different level. When a finance YouTuber or any influencer comes online during market hours, there is a decent size of subscribers who watch that stream. I have seen 25,000 people or even sometimes 50,000 watching a livestream.

Can you guess why they are really doing so?

Parallel trading. All of them want to trade in the security or stock that is going to be recommended in the livestream.

Do you think that's ethical or legal?

Well, it's definitely not ethical and in terms of legality it sits in the same space where no one knows the real agenda, as we discussed earlier. It's not that every finfluencer who goes live or does a video has a hidden agenda. But why get to places that are patchy?

The stock market is a place where one can make a decent amount of money over time but you need to be cautious—as a trader, as an investor, as a businessman, or as a content creator.

By the time you read this, SEBI has already passed a circular that brings an illegitimacy to any form of live stock market trading on YouTube. In fact, any analysis of a stock done on social media must be done on the chart or data which is at least three months old.

This reminds me of one of the complaints against one such finfluencer who was crossing a big line. He was breaking all of SEBI's rules and regulations.

We decided to act against that. We investigated. We complained. We waited.

Then SEBI penalized the person. Yes, we are talking about none other than Baap of Charts.

Let's talk at length about how we went about investigating this person.

11

HOW WE INVESTIGATED BAAP OF CHARTS

It was a regular Monday afternoon in March 2023. I had just had lunch and was feeling a bit drowsy. I thought I'd quickly go online and I saw this post on X (formerly Twitter):

> I have made an algo which will double your capital in 10 weeks. How many of you are interested? Let's kick it off this Holi!

The handle name was Md. Nasir. I reposted it and tagged SEBI and NSE (National Stock Exchange).

I was a bit taken aback since this was clearly a violation and no one can claim something like this. The strangest part was that he was doing it all in the open. There was a website, a YouTube channel, an Instagram handle and a Telegram channel.

I waited for a few days after the retweet. Nothing really happened. I thought someone from the regulator might talk about it or send an advisory email in the public's general interest.

Something? Anything!

But there was nothing. I could not wait.

A few days later, on 22 March 2023, as soon as I reached my office I told our creative head, Ashish, 'Let's do a video on this Baap of Chart guy! Nobody seems to care.'

'Sure, but since all this is happening on X, I think we should keep it on that platform for now and not take it up on YouTube,' Ashish said.

'Sure. But we need a video!'

We shot the video, edited it the same day and published it on X around 8 p.m.[21]

Everyone including SEBI, NSE, BSE, and the brokers' association ANMI (Association of National Exchanges Members of India) was tagged. We even tagged the finance ministry. However, I wasn't happy with the reach of the video. Obviously, this message needed to reach a wider audience. Interestingly, four days later, the original post by Md. Nasir was deleted.

I posted again.

For a few days, I thought maybe the person had realized the direction he was going in and would stop indulging in illegalities. In the following week, I looked at his website. There was so much phoney stuff:

- Guaranteed returns
- Illegal portfolio management and profit sharing
- Tips without a SEBI RA licence
- Some algo software that had nothing to do with actual algorithms

As mentioned earlier, our videos have a complaint form for people who have been scammed. Out of the nearly 3,000 complaints we had received in the one year before this, more than 50 were against Baap of Charts. The person was unstoppable in conning people.

I had a closer look at his YouTube channel and found that some of the topics were unreal. If a new trader looked at some

[21]A Digital Blogger/Aseem Juneja (@adigitalblogger), 'We have never done this before…', *X*, *22* March 2023, https://tinyurl.com/8a3uvsvw. Accessed on 3 March 2025.

of his video thumbnails on YouTube, there was a high chance of falling in his trap.

Here is a quick look:

This is nothing but inducement in SEBI's regulatory terms. Here's what Md. Nasir was doing:

- Unrealistic messaging was being thrown at subscribers to make them think all this was a possibility.
- A FOMO (fear of missing out) effect was being created in the mind of a budding trader.
- One of the most gullible persons in stock market is someone who has lost money in trading, because they always want to recover their losses. He was targeting such people too.

We waited for another two months. Then I thought, what the hell.

I went to the Baap of Charts website. There were too many plans to choose from:

- **Buy BoC (Baap of Chart) Algo:** This was a mix of a few setups placed on a third-party software called Tradetron. It had nothing to do with algo trading and even if it had, there was no approval taken from the exchange (NSE). This approval is mandatory.
  Cost: ₹9,000 for positional, intraday and option selling in a single pack
- **BoC D 30:** A profit plan, where a 100 per cent guarantee of 30 per cent profit on a daily basis was given. The words 'guarantee' or 'assurance' are a big no in SEBI books. I bought this plan and all I got were some tips shared in a WhatsApp group. Cost: ₹6,000
- **Loss-recovery strategy:** A guarantee of ₹3 lakh to ₹6 lakh profit on a capital of ₹3 lakh to ₹10 lakh on the expiry day was being offered. This implies a profit of 30 per cent to 100 per cent in a single day.

Of course, when one is talking to loss-making traders, it becomes much easier to sell if you sell like this. It is both unethical and illegal.

I bought the BoC D 30 plan, paying ₹6,000 for something I didn't really need. But sometimes one does something they are passionate about, with no idea where it will go.

One interesting thing was that this person who had glamourized the stock market scene—with people having fan moments with him, with seminars and workshops being held in five-star resorts and hotel chains—had no payment gateway or any other transaction mechanism except a direct UPI payment to his phone number.

I made the payment. Nothing happened. No message, no email, no call.

'Well, is this the whole scam?' I thought. I sent an email the same day and a reminder the next day.

Three days later, I sent another reminder. This time I mentioned that I would be sending a report to SEBI if I didn't get a response. Still nothing. Four days later, I sent yet another reminder. Then, I finally I got a three-word response saying, 'WhatsApp on 8700XXXXXX.' This response meant that there was a slight chance the person might not be a scammer, and just does all this unintentionally.

My hopes were crushed the same day when I was added to a WhatsApp announcement group and started getting all these messages:

'Sir, he is an absolute fraud. How can he share all these tips without a SEBI RA licence?' Ashish said.

'No doubt,' I responded. 'Let's plan a whole script on this. Call Amrit to join the meeting.'

One good thing with all of us working together is that the whole team stays aware of new sorts of frauds or violations. Most of my team members feel there is almost no likelihood that they or their friends and family can ever be scammed in stock market frauds.

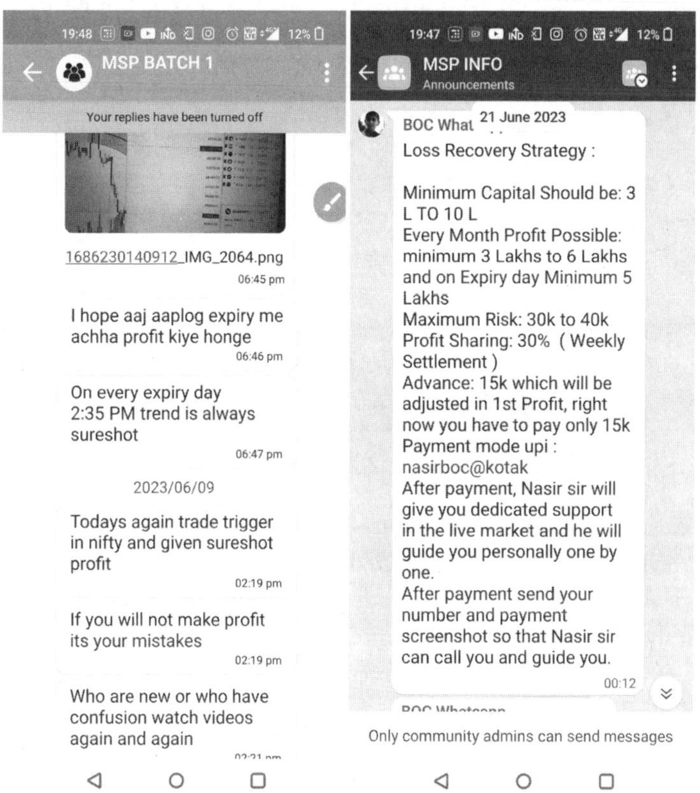

We worked on the script that day. It was 21 June 2023 when we received the tips on WhatsApp. In the next one week, we scripted, produced and edited the video. We also did one more thing. On 29 June 2023, I wrote to SEBI and shared documents, screenshots, screen-recordings and everything else we had access to. Along with the email, there were three attachments we used as proof of the allegations made. These were screenshots of a broadcast messaging service in Baap of Chart's app discussing market entry levels, capital to be deployed, expected returns, share of profits he would charge, trade quantity and a lot more.

These later became part of the SEBI order.

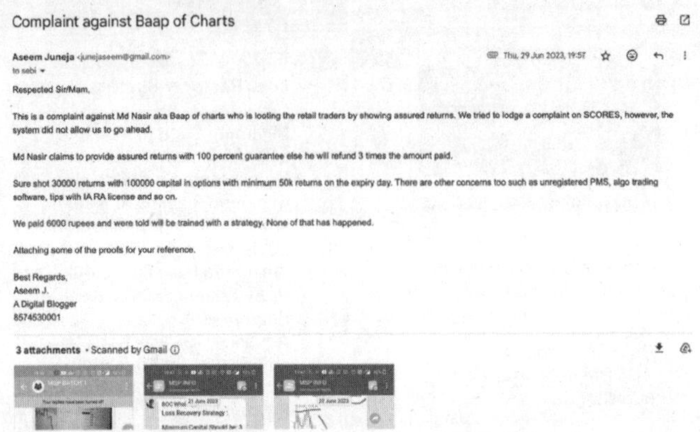

Complaint against Baap of Charts

Aseem Juneja <junejaseem@gmail.com> Thu, 29 Jun 2023, 19:57
to sebi

Respected Sir/Mam,

This is a complaint against Md Nasir aka Baap of charts who is looting the retail traders by showing assured returns. We tried to lodge a complaint on SCORES, however, the system did not allow us to go ahead.

Md Nasir claims to provide assured returns with 100 percent guarantee else he will refund 3 times the amount paid.

Sure shot 30000 returns with 100000 capital in options with minimum 50k returns on the expiry day. There are other concerns too such as unregistered PMS, algo trading software, tips with IA RA license and so on.

We paid 6000 rupees and were told will be trained with a strategy. None of that has happened.

Attaching some of the proofs for your reference.

Best Regards,
Aseem J.
A Digital Blogger
8574530001

3 attachments · Scanned by Gmail

We went all out, so on 5 July 2023 we published our video on YouTube. It got an unexpected response. We had over 400,000 views. Many viewers seconded the thought of him being a fraudster based on their own experiences.

'We have done what we could have done,' we thought and moved on. We had limited expectations that anything would happen. In the next few months, we worked on a few more cases of scams and frauds.

And then came THE day. It was a Friday—25 October 2023.

I was going to leave early from office. It was my cousin's wedding on the weekend and I was supposed to drive for 4–5 hours that evening. Almost everyone but the creative team had left the office already.

I have a daily habit of checking SEBI's website 15–20 times to see if there's anything new. I checked the website as usual before I left.

> Interim order cum SCN in the matter of unregistered investment advisory activities of Mohammad Nasiruddin Ansari/Baap of Chart!

Really?

I clicked the link. It was a 45-page PDF document. I kept scrolling. If anyone is penalized, it's mentioned right at the bottom of such orders. At the end of the document, among the thousands of words, I saw a figure.

> ₹172,076,616.09 (Rupees Seventeen Crore Twenty Lakh Seventy-Six Thousand Six Hundred Sixteen and Nine Paisa)

This is the how much Baap of Chart made in illegal gains over the two-year inspection period. This amount would be impounded by SEBI.

Wow.

I had paid him ₹6,000. Thousands like me must have paid him this amount and more. Crores of capital must have been lost by investors and traders following his ridiculous strategies. Justice was served.

'Ashish, Amrit!' I shouted as I read the order. 'Let's shoot a video!'

Ashish came running in.

'What happened, sir?' he asked.

'Baap of Chart is being penalized by SEBI. 17 crore!' I exclaimed.

Ashish sat down on the floor and exclaimed, 'What!' He then immediately stood up and ran out of the room.

'Where are you going?' I shouted again.

'I'm getting a camera, tripod and mic. Let's make a video,' he responded.

Amrit and I started laughing.

'But there is no script and don't you have to leave? It's already 7.30 p.m.,' Ashish asked me after he came back with the equipment.

'Yes, but I will be back on Monday and that will be too late. Can you edit this in two hours if I give you the raw video in the next 20 minutes?' I asked.

'I can try. We can do a basic edit but how will you shoot the video in 20 minutes? There is no script,' he replied.

'I know the man, the case and the penalty clauses by heart. I will also skim the rest of the order and mark its major parts. SEBI also used our email and proof to pass this order!' I said excitedly.

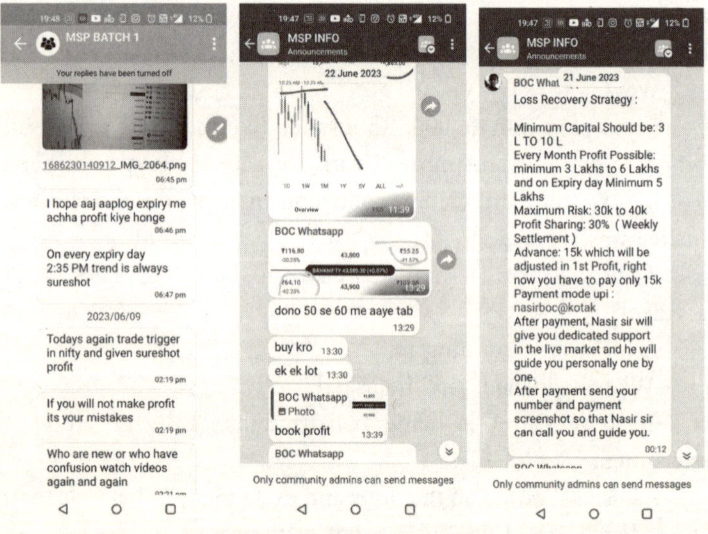

'Oh my god, really? The video must go out tonight, sir,' Amrit said this time.

I shot the video in the next 25 minutes and it went for an edit. At 10.15 p.m., the video was published. It took the traders' community by storm. In the first three hours, 100,000 viewers had seen the video. People were happy and amazed that SEBI took this much-needed action.

A large chunk of fake-finfluencers did not sleep that night.

Thankfully my family was patient and waited for me to finish. A few hours later, we were driving to the wedding and I said to myself, 'I am going to make more of these. This fake-finfluencer series will make a difference. I am glad this happened.'

'Who are you talking to?' my wife asked from the back seat.

'Nothing. I was just thinking about a video.'

Till date, that video has been seen by over 800,000 viewers. While that doesn't seem like a big number in comparison to the millions of views that comedy or political videos get, that one order from SEBI changed the lives of many people, not just Md. Nasir's.

After all this, what if you do end up becoming a victim to such a fake-finfluencer. What can you do about such a person? How can you file a complaint? Is it easy or impossible?

Read on to empower yourself with the needed information.

12

HOW TO FILE A COMPLAINT AGAINST A FAKE-FINFLUENCER

We get so many comments on our channel from people who have been defrauded by a finfluencer or someone who is not SEBI-registered.

I have been robbed of ₹5 lakh by a YouTuber. Can you help?

He promised me via Instagram DM that he would give me 20 per cent returns every day. I invested ₹10 lakh and now he is not responding to me. What can I do?

I was part of a 'premium' Telegram channel after paying ₹5,000 for tips. Then I lost ₹2.5 lakh by trading on them. What to do?

To file a complaint at SEBI, the regulator has a portal called SCORES that can be accessed via scores.gov.in. The complaint can also be submitted for grievance redressal at another portal called SmartODR (smartodr.in).

But there is a speed breaker here. These two portals—SCORES and Smart ODR—only allow complaints against entities that are SEBI-registered, including stockbrokers, research analysts, advisors, portfolio managers and others.

So, what can you do when someone unregistered with SEBI defrauds you, like a finfluencer? And what kind of frauds are we talking about?

- Giving tips without RA licence
- Demat account handling on a profit-sharing basis
- Providing investment schemes with guaranteed returns
- Anything that has not been committed by a SEBI-registered entity

If you have made a payment and have been defrauded by such unregistered fake finfluencers, then you need to start by collecting proof.

These could be WhatsApp screenshots showing tips shared, screen or call recordings, documentation shared, payment-transaction screenshots, emails, attachments, etc. All of this should be attached and linked in an email that you send to SEBI at sebi@sebi.gov.in.

I should warn you that this is not a sure-shot solution. At best, this is an attempt. There is no 100 per cent guarantee that this will be picked up by an official at SEBI. Furthermore, even if it is picked up, it will take time, from months to even years. You can call yourself lucky if the issue is resolved in a few months. Remember, it is not really SEBI's duty to get involved in a case which is not directly under its regulations. If you look at it dispassionately, you have actually been defrauded under IPC 420. The police and the courts are the ones who could actually help.

Once you file the complaint through email, it remains to be seen whether SEBI really wants to get involved.

What if there are issues with your email and it gets rejected because you sent out incomplete information? Let's frame a complaint.

Here are some pointers:

1. **Introduction:** Briefly introduce yourself, then talk about the person you are complaining against and what the

complaint is about. It must not take more than two to three lines.

2. **Details of the fraudster:** Talk about the fake finfluencer at length. Explain their social media reach across platforms, the wrongs they have committed, and explain the modus operandi in detail.
3. **Scale of the fraud:** Here talk numbers and money. Explain the scale of the overall fraud being committed by the person so that the regulator understands the depth of the matter. I'll discuss how to calculate this later in the chapter.
4. **Proof:** No court will allow you to file a case without proof or witnesses. This is where you detail the attachments or links you will add in the email to SEBI. You must list these down and simplify the meaning of what you are submitting so that there is no room for confusion. I have noted earlier that these can include transaction-history screenshots, payment screenshots, Telegram tips, WhatsApp conversations, email communications, website links, documents shared, and anything else in the same vein.
5. **Attachments:** No matter what happens, do not—I repeat, do not—miss out on this. Furthermore, make sure to properly title every image or document so that it is easily understandable by anyone.

Always proofread your final email before you send it.

Here's one such actual email we sent to SEBI so you can understand the structure and language. Use this for reference and remember to craft your own complaints because every situation is different.

Hello Sir/Ma'am,

This is regarding a YouTuber/Instagram fake finfluencer named Devansh Rai. He is an unregistered RA who is giving tips and recommendations in lieu of paid consideration.

1. Who is He?

As stated, the person goes by the name of Devansh Rai and has the following social media presence:

YouTube	**Followers: 468k**	https://www.YouTube.com/@DevanshRai
Instagram	**Followers: 268k**	https://www.instagram.com/devanshrai-yt/
Telegram	**Followers: 81k**	https://web.telegram.org/a/#-1001763413616 or @tradewithdevanshrai

He offers a subscription to a premium Telegram channel where daily tips and levels are provided. The person admits he is not a SEBI-registered research analyst and still chooses to violate the same regulation.

2. How Was He Caught?

- I became one of his clients to validate the above and to do so:
- I watched one of his YouTube videos where he shared his free Telegram channel link:
- https://web.telegram.org/a/#-1001763413616
- On this channel, he puts a payment link for becoming part of his 'premium mentorship' programme:
- https://web.fankonnect.com/g/1504
- He offers 2 plans: monthly ₹4,999 and quarterly ₹13,000
- He provided a coupon code for a discount of

₹1,000 and I paid ₹3,999 for his monthly 'premium mentorship'.

- I became part of another Telegram channel that had 583 members.
- The person shares a YouTube live link every morning and gives tips and levels.
- After some time, he removes the video from YouTube and the link from the Telegram channel.
- This livestream happens on his main YouTube channel.
- We have downloaded some and shared the clips where he is asking paid members to place a trade. He provides buy-and-sell signals along with the stop loss and target price. There is no education happening in these sessions.
- Apart from the live YouTube sessions, nothing else happens in the mentorship Telegram channel.

3. Scale of the Fraud

When I joined his premium Telegram channel, I found there were other 583 paying members.

As mentioned above, I ended up paying him about ₹4,000. Assuming everyone paid ₹4,000–₹5,000 to get into the group for one month, the person must have made around ₹23.32 lakh to ₹29.15 lakh in a month. He has been doing this for a while now.

Devansh Rai is clearly violating SEBI (RA) Regulations 2014 Section 3 (1).

4. Proof

1. Here are the details on the payments made:

Sl no.	Date	Amount	Narration	Counterparty bank account details (name and number)
1	27 Feb 2024	₹3,999	Empty	Takes payment through a third-party platform named Fabconnect. Attached screenshots of bank account details: 1. Devansh Rai Free Telegram.png 2. Devansh Rai Payment Page.png 3. Devansh Rai Payment Method.png We made the payment and attached are the bank and Fabconnect confirmation screenshots. 1. Devansh Rai Payment Bank.png 2. Devansh Rai Payment Confirmation.png

2. This payment link is shared on his Telegram channel.
3. We received a payment confirmation once it was made.
4. I was then entered into the 'premium Telegram group' where tips were shared. Members also got a private YouTube link where trades were provided between 9.15 a.m. and 10 a.m. every morning.
5. Specific trade entries and exits were given during the private YouTube live sessions (tips in Telegram proof).
   Devansh Rai Telegram Tips.png
   Devansh Rai Tips Telegram.png
   Devansh Rai Private YouTube Link.png
   Tips screen recordings proof: Video recording of his YouTube Live shared privately with the paid members only (Devansh Rai YT Live Tips.mp4)

6. Contact information:
   Telegram channel Links:
   Free: https://web.telegram.org/a/#-1001763413616
   Paid: https://web.telegram.org/a/#-1001805548068
   (might not be accessible to non-members, screenshot attached)

I hope this reaches the right person at SEBI who can set an example for other unregistered advisors such as this one. Hopefully, this will be enough. Please let me know if any further assistance is required.

Thanks,
Aseem J.

Once you have sent this email, you need to wait.

For how long?

There is no fixed answer. It may take a few weeks to a few months. But make sure to add a reminder to the sent email every two weeks. There is also a possibility that you may get a template-based email that says something like this:

Dear Sir/Madam,

This is with reference to the trailing mail.
Please lodge your complaint on SEBI Complaints Redress System (SCORES) at https://scores.sebi.gov.in/ or SEBI SCORES Mobile App which is available on both Apple App Store and Google Play Store.

Please note that as per circular No. SEBI/HO/OIAE/IGRD/CIR/P/2023/156 dated 20 September 2023, investors who wish to lodge a complaint are required to register themselves on SCORES before lodging the complaint against a listed company, a SEBI-registered intermediary or a SEBI-recognized Market Infrastructure Institution. While

> registering the complaints, mandatory details like name of the investor, address, PAN, mobile number and e-mail ID need to be provided for registration.
>
> SCORES aids in tracking the status of the complaints any time by the investor while also providing notifications from time to time with respect to their complaints. Complaints lodged on the SCORES Portal or SCORES mobile app help in keeping a proper audit trail of the complaint which is essential for future reference. In view of the same, complaints sent through e-mails shall not be processed.
>
> For any help in lodging a complaint on SCORES or with respect to your complaints, please contact the SEBI Toll-Free Helpline number 1800 266 7575 or 1800 22 7575.
>
> For any technical assistance please send an email on scoreshelp@sebi.gov.in or call us at 022-2644-9377/022-4045-9377/022-207.

In this case, you need to send another email as a response, saying the entity you are complaining against is not a SEBI-registered entity but is mis-selling SEBI-registered products and asset classes or is violating SEBI rules and regulations.

You need to realize that pulling something like this off—even with time and patience—will not be easy. This is why it is very important for you to know that in the first place you will be much better off not getting involved in anything that is not directly under SEBI.

Let's say you get lucky and SEBI decides to go ahead with your complaint. This is how they will respond to your complaint email:

In this case, someone from SEBI will email you—i.e., an actual person instead of a robotic response.

They will ask for a few details such as:

- Payment amount, transaction and bank details
- Emails, WhatsApp and SMS screenshots
- Call recordings and mobile numbers used
- Any agreements and copies of tips.

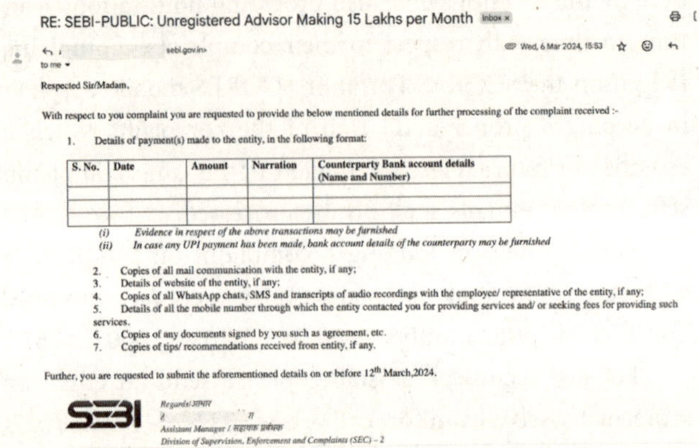

RE: SEBI-PUBLIC: Unregistered Advisor Making 15 Lakhs per Month Inbox ×

sebi.gov.in> Wed, 6 Mar 2024, 15:53

to me

Respected Sir/Madam,

With respect to you complaint you are requested to provide the below mentioned details for further processing of the complaint received :-

1. Details of payment(s) made to the entity, in the following format:

S. No.	Date	Amount	Narration	Counterparty Bank account details (Name and Number)

(i) *Evidence in respect of the above transactions may be furnished*

(ii) *In case any UPI payment has been made, bank account details of the counterparty may be furnished*

2. Copies of all mail communication with the entity, if any;
3. Details of website of the entity, if any;
4. Copies of all WhatsApp chats, SMS and transcripts of audio recordings with the employee/ representative of the entity, if any;
5. Details of all the mobile number through which the entity contacted you for providing services and/ or seeking fees for providing such services.
6. Copies of any documents signed by you such as agreement, etc.
7. Copies of tips/ recommendations received from entity, if any.

Further, you are requested to submit the aforementioned details on or before 12th March,2024.

Regards/आभार

Assistant Manager / सहायक प्रबंधक

Division of Supervision, Enforcement and Complaints (SEC) – 2

This is a good signal that the case has gone into investigation stage and someone at SEBI is looking into it.

The same email template and formalities can be used in case you have been defrauded by an unregistered tip provider, a research company, a profit-sharing fraudster, some Ponzi scheme, etc. If your proof and documents are genuine, SEBI will pass an order against the guilty even if it takes its own sweet time. All you have to do is wait for the magic to happen.

While it's better not to get caught in a scam in the first place, sometimes even a SEBI-registered stockbroker can get you in trouble. It's rare but it may happen. Wouldn't it be better if you can identify a crook stockbroker on your own? Won't you feel safe that the stockbroker you have chosen has one of the lowest chances of bringing you trouble?

Let's discuss how to objectively identify a stockbroker that brings you the least concern.

Part 4

STOCKBROKER FRAUDS

13

HOW TO IDENTIFY A CROOK STOCKBROKER

There are always bad apples. In the same way, out of hundreds of clean and honest SEBI-registered stockbrokers, there will be a few that end up as bad apples. Such stockbrokers are not just harmful to their own clients, but also to the whole industry in general.

Let me walk you through a case where we assisted one of our subscribers, a senior citizen named Shashi Kumar (name changed), involved with a renowned stockbroker, Sure Securities (name changed).

'Sir, you can buy a subscription to our exclusive PRS Scheme,' Ravi (name changed), a sales executive at Sure Securities, said to Shashi Kumar.

Shashi had recently opened a demat account with Sure Securities, a broking arm of Sure Bank. He was working in Egypt and had come back home on a holiday.

'What PRS? I don't understand these technical terms,' Shashi responded.

'Sir, don't worry, I will explain. It's my job to get you the best returns,' Ravi said in the cheesiest way possible. 'PRS stands for premium research service. It is operated by the top research analyst team of Sure Securities.'

'What would it cost me? And what are its benefits?'

'Sir, you will get a research strategy from us along with a recommendation. This will help you make a 20 per cent annual return. What is your capital amount?'

'₹25 lakh. 20 per cent would mean I will make ₹5 lakh a year?' Shashi wanted to be absolutely sure.

'More or less, sir,' Ravi responded. He was under pressure to meet his targets. He was nowhere close to his monthly target but this sale could turn everything around and he might even make a decent incentive.

'Okay, you can call me tomorrow and I will confirm,' Shashi said, wanting to buy some time.

'Sir, we have been interacting for a while now. I think you can trust me. You will make decent returns; all my clients would agree,' Ravi tried again.

'Okay. Let's go ahead,' Shashi agreed, albeit a bit uncertainly. He barely knew Ravi but the latter had been calling him ever since he landed in the city.

'Great, sir. I will email you a PDF document. Print it out, fill in some details with your signatures, and I will complete the rest of the formalities. Have a good day,' Ravi concluded, while trying not to jump with joy.

Apart from all other terms and conditions in the PRS Scheme Ravi was selling, there were these ones as well:

- Sure Securities can, at any given point in time, change this plan, create a new one and shift Shashi into that one or remove the plan altogether.
- PRS is not an exchange-approved plan and if there is any dispute the client may have, he will not approach any of the complaint redressal mechanisms provided by the regulator.
- The client, if dissatisfied with the scheme, cannot hold

> Sure Securities, its research analysts, directors, officers, employees and associates responsible for any actions, claims, demands, losses, damages, costs, charges and expenses which he may suffer, sustain or incur by way of the above offer i.e. the PRS Scheme.

Can it get more ridiculous than this? There were 15 more such terms and conditions that only took care of Sure Securities and put no burden or responsibility for the PRS Scheme on the broker.

Thus, in a sense, the broker was offering an unapproved recommendation-based 'strategy' placed at a cost of ₹1.25 lakh + GST (around ₹1.5 lakh) and was taking no responsibility for the outcome. The plan could be changed at any given point at the broker's discretion. Also, why was the executive (Ravi, in this case) trying to take care of his monthly sales targets and telling the client that this PRS Scheme could offer as high as 20 per cent yearly returns? There were assurances being given in the sales pitch. Unethical and illegal.

SEBI has clear guidelines on mutual funds or algo-trading platforms as per which brokers are not allowed to use past performance of the products to market future returns. The same rule must be applied here. As far as a PRS Scheme is concerned, it is clearly made to make money for the broker. The tips and recommendations from the broker's research analysts, which no one seems to be interested in, are being sold in an intelligent-seeming package with a label such as PRS. On top of that, it's not even approved by any regulatory body.

There is also a possibility that Sure Securities, or other brokers who are running such schemes, is doing so without the knowledge of the exchanges or the regulator.

Here you are, looking for a perfect stockbroker who takes care of your investments and returns in the future. But it's unrealistic to want a broker whose app never crashes, whose customer support is top-notch, whose brokerage charges are the lowest in the industry, and so on. Eventually, you need to understand that stockbrokers are businesses run by humans, and as we know, 'to err is human!'

This is applicable to trading across the globe. It's also not the case that only Indian stockbrokers have their share of problems. Some charge extra money, some might just stop working, some might not pick up your call when you need them the most, and it goes on. At the same time, a lot depends on you. Like I mentioned earlier, you will not find the perfect someone, so if mistakes are made, you ideally should be ready to let go.

For instance, some of you might not need regular customer support. So, would you be okay if your broker is bad at answering your calls? Others might be willing to pay a higher brokerage as they are getting top-class support from the service team, or the research team is helping their clients get magnified profits.

Now let's understand how you can take care of yourself while finding a stockbroker.

There are around five crore active demat accounts in India.[22] An active demat account is one that has placed at least one trade in the last six months. These demat accounts are opened through multiple stockbrokers. For instance, Zerodha had 7,287,148 accounts, Groww had 9,538,609, Angel One had 6,111,879, and ICICI Securities had 1,845,202 till March 2024.

But why are we talking about demat accounts?

Well, if there are people with demat accounts, some of them will also have complaints. If there is a pattern of complaints in these demat accounts, then you may get an idea about what kind

[22] 'Report 1C: Report of Redressal of Complaints Lodged by Clients Against Trading Members (TMs) during 2024–25', last updated on 31 January 2025, National Stock Exchange of India, https://tinyurl.com/2kyh2rnu. Accessed on 3 March 2025.

of complaints a specific broker gets the most.

But before we discuss examples of brokers with complaints, let us understand the type of complaints a client may have with the stockbroker. This may get a bit technical but stay with me.

There are 9 types of complaints:

I Non-receipt/delay in payment
   a. Delay in payment
   b. Non-receipt of payment
   c. Delay in refund of margin payment
   d. Non-settlement of accounts

II Non-receipt/delay in securities
   a. Delay in delivery
   b. Non-receipt of delivery
   c. Delay in refund of margin deposit
   d. Non-settlement of accounts

III Non-receipt of documents
   a. Contract notes
   b. Bills
   c. Account statements
   d. Agreement copies

IV Unauthorized trades/misappropriation
   a. Unauthorized trades in the client account
   b. Misappropriation of funds/securities

V Service-related
   a. Excess brokerage
   b. Non-execution of order
   c. Wrong execution of order
   d. Connectivity/system-related problem
   e. Non-receipt of corporate benefits
   f. Other service defaults

VI Closing out/squaring up
   a. Closing off/squaring up position without consent
   b. Dispute in auction value/close-out value

VII Non-implementation of arbitration award

VIII IPO-related

IX Others

Let me simplify this further:

1. Type 1 is primarily filed when the broker is taking time or not completing settlements of the pending payments of different forms to your trading account.
2. Type 2 is about a delay in securities not being reflected in your demat account.
3. Type 3 is when the broker delays administrative work, i.e. documentation.
4. Type 4 is relatively serious when the brokers or sub-brokers are placing unauthorized trades, i.e. trading in the accounts of the client without taking any confirmation.
5. Type 5 is majorly about issues around trading app problems, hidden charges applied by the broker, or anything related to the services provided.
6. Type 6 happens when the trading app closes the running trade position of the trader without any intimation.
7. Type 7 is applied when the client has won a case against the broker in a complaint at NSE or SEBI and the broker has been penalized an amount that they have failed to pay to the client.
8. Type 8 is anything related to IPO subscriptions.
9. For anything else that is an issue, Type 9 works.

Let's understand which of the top stockbrokers have received how many complaints in one financial year and what percentage of complaints fall in what type of category. Apart from the types of complaints, we also need to know the total complaints lodged against the broker along with the percentage of active clients filing those complaints.

The table on the following page gives a quick overview.

For instance, the 1,202 complaints for Angel One may look the highest among all, but it also has a larger active client base, which takes the complaint percentage to as low as 0.01 per cent. Then there is Finvasia, whose complaint percentage is almost 100 times larger than Angel One, sitting at a value of 0.97 per cent. The reason for such a high complaint percentage is the relatively larger number of complaints filed with respect to the total number of clients the stockbroker has.

From the given table, here are some observations:

- If you are expecting top services from the broker, Upstox may not be a top choice.
- Motilal might not be good for sharing credentials with the sub-broking team. ICICI Securities does not seem to be doing a good job when it comes to settling payments of client accounts.
- Zerodha and Upstox don't have issues around unauthorized trading, while Angel One is smooth when it comes to any documentation or administrative aspects.

So, this is how you try to find out the right stockbroker for your needs. You need to make some quick observations with data collected over a year for a good idea about who is a good fit.

However, if you do get stuck with a broker over any issue, you will need to know how to sort that out and go through the whole process of filing a complaint with the regulator.

Let's discuss the kinds of issues one can face before that.

Broker Name	Total Complaints	Complaint per centage	Type 1	Type 2	Type 3	Type 4	Type 5	Type 6	Type 7	Type 8	Type 9
Angel One	1,202	0.01 per cent	7.8 per cent	-	0.4 per cent	11.5 per cent	61.1 per cent	-	-	-	19.1 per cent
Zerodha	567	0.007 per cent	6.5 per cent	-	1 per cent	7.2 per cent	62 per cent	-	-	0.17 per cent	22.2 per cent
Motilal Oswal	505	0.05 per cent	3.16 per cent	-	0.8 per cent	33.4 per cent	45.5 per cent	-	-	0.20 per cent	16.8 per cent
ICICI Securities	971	0.05 per cent	16 per cent	-	0.6 per cent	10.1 per cent	53.4 per cent	-	-	-	19.6 per cent
Finvasia	1,110	0.97 per cent	12 per cent	-	2 per cent	21 per cent	57.7 per cent	-	-	-	7 per cent
Upstox	299	0.01 per cent	7.3 per cent	-	1.3 per cent	7.3 per cent	66.5 per cent	-	-	0.3 per cent	17 per cent

Source: *NSE 1C Report*

14

TYPES OF STOCKBROKER FRAUDS

Indians lost more than ₹1,750 crore to cyber criminals in the first four months of 2024, with over 7.4 lakh cybercrime complaints being registered on the National Cybercrime Reporting Portal between January and April 2024. About 85 per cent of these were online financial frauds.[23] We have talked about financial frauds by unregulated entities. In this chapter, our focus is on stockbrokers.

To begin with, as of today the top 10 stockbrokers control 83 per cent of the overall active demat accounts in the country. There are more than 500 stockbrokers overall. That means around 17 per cent of the total demat accounts are handled by hundreds of other stockbrokers. In a general sense, there is not a lot of money for these stockbrokers to make from these miniscule numbers. There is another interesting part to this. Around 39 stockbrokers have been expelled by SEBI in the last five years and most scams or frauds have generally been done by brokers outside of the top 10.

There is another way to look at it. If we go from the retail traders' side, there were 10,628 complaints raised by traders in the financial year 2023–24. Out of them, Angel One had 1,203,

---

[23]Tripathi, Rahul, 'Indians Lost Over ₹1,750 Crore to Cyber Fraud in First Four Months of 2024', *The Economic Times*, 27 May 2024, https://tinyurl.com/bp9v3dk8. Accessed on 3 March 2025.

Finvasia had 1,110, ICICI Securities had 971, and so on.

You may think that the more complaints a broker has, the worse it is.

But that's not really how it is.

A better yardstick for a broker's performance is not the number of complaints but the percentage of complaints out of the total active client base the broker has. So, a stockbroker with a large number of active demat accounts will have a relatively smaller percentage of complaints.

From that angle, for the same financial year, Finvasia had 0.97 per cent of its clients complaining, Mandot Securities had 0.70 per cent, and mStock had 0.14 per cent. Angel One, in fact, had a complaint percentage of 0.01 per cent, while ICICI Securities sat at 0.05 per cent. The industry average of complaint percentage for the whole year across stockbrokers was 0.02 per cent.

Now don't look at the absolute numbers but the percentage. What do these numbers convert to in terms of stock market frauds? There is no direct correlation of complaints and stockbroker fraud but you can get an objective sense before falling for a marketing advertisement.

What Is Stockbroker Fraud?

Anything a broker or its team does to you or your trading account without your knowledge that brings a loss of money or mental peace is a stockbroker fraud. While there are nine kinds of complaints a retail investor can officially file, the types vary. To simplify, we have segregated a majority of the kinds of frauds into four categories:

1. Brokerage churning through tips
2. Excess brokerage/charges

3. Trading app glitches
4. Unauthorized trades/misusing client funds

There could be other kinds of fraud but these are the ones that happen the most.

Brokerage churning

Let's illustrate this with an example. Let's say a new trader, Viren, opens a new demat account and he starts getting calls from the research or advisory team of the stockbroker.

'Hello, sir. I see you have an account with us. I am Ankush, your relationship manager (RM) and my job is to help you find the right stocks and securities to trade.'

'Okay, and how much will you charge for this?' Viren asks.

'This is absolutely free.'

'Really? So what am I supposed to do?'

'Nothing much. Since we are a SEBI-registered full-service stockbroker and have an RA licence as well, I will be providing you tips every morning and afternoon on a daily basis. You can use them to trade using our trading app,' Ankush responds.

'Wow, I don't need to pay ₹25,000 to the advisory that called me yesterday for tips. These people are giving me the same thing for free,' Viren thinks to himself.

'Okay, let's do it, Ankush,' he responds.

Like most people, Viren has no idea about Ankush's hidden interests in this call. By giving you tips for free, they are getting you to trade from your newly-opened account. When you trade, there will be a brokerage amount you need to pay. That brokerage is revenue for the stockbroker—one of their biggest sources of income.

For some of these stockbrokers, research advisors don't care for your profits as much as the brokerage targets they need to wring out of you. You will be astonished to know that one such sales executive working with a stockbroker in the salary range of ₹15,000 to ₹25,000 per month gets brokerage revenue targets as high as ₹50,000 to ₹100,000. If you earn more than that, there are lavish incentives to be made. Apart from opening demat accounts and getting the margin added, they are supposed to get a particular number of trades done from the accounts opened in the whole month.

For Ankush, two to three months of average performance is enough for him to be kicked out of the company. So the pressure of getting the brokerage is huge. The livelihood of such executives depends on the number of trades you place. What would they care for more? Your eventual profits or the number of trades you do and the brokerage you eventually pay to the stockbroker?

Let me walk you through a real-life example.

This is the case of Mr Mittal (name changed) from Mumbai which was arbitrated under SEBI redressals. SEBI passed an order in his favour after understanding the case.

He and his wife are senior citizens and worked hard their whole lives. Mr Mittal was financially aware to the extent that he had kept a stock market portfolio for the last 19 to 20 years. The couple had demat accounts with HDFC Securities and SHCIL, with a combined portfolio value of around ₹30 lakh to ₹35 lakh.

One day, they got a call from a local sub-broker named Abhijit Dawar (name changed) working under a stockbroker named Doll Money (name changed).[24]

'Sir, we would like you to open a demat account with us. When can we visit?'

Mr Mittal wasn't keen but after regular calls from the sub-

[24]'A.M. NO. NSEWRO/0017373/20-21/ISC/IGRP/ARB', National Stock Exchange, https://tinyurl.com/yt2kfdy4. Accessed on 3 March 2025.

broker, he allowed him to come home. Abhijit convinced Mr Mittal that he was killing his money and could have saved more if he was there to guide him. It did not take him long to convince Mr Mittal to transfer his shares from his existing demat account to a new one with Doll Money.

The Doll Money sub-broker got around 40 signatures across multiple forms, Mr Mittal said in his complaint to SEBI and NSE later. After the shares were transferred, Mr Mittal started getting calls from Abhijit from a different number that generally went like this:

'Mittal*ji*, I have got some recommendations for you that can get your portfolio a decent profit. I am going to call you from the official number and ask you "Shall I go ahead with the trade", and you just have to say "yes" in the call.'

'But Abhijit, I don't want to take on so much risk on my portfolio. All the trades must be in stocks and equity only,' Mr Mittal reminded him.

'Sir, you know me. We live in the same township, the same locality. I understand your concerns and I am here to get the best profits for you. Just say yes in the next call I am making,' Abhijit said this in the local Marathi dialect to prove his trustworthiness.

'Umm…okay,' Mr Mittal responded, without understanding much about what was going on.

Abhijit would then call again and get a yes from Mr Mittal.

What exactly was happening?

Mr Mittal learned much later that his and the wife's portfolio of ₹35 lakh was reduced to a mere ₹5 to ₹7 lakh. Every other penny in their trading accounts was gone.

Gone where? In losses mostly.

But it also went to Doll Money's bank account. How? As brokerage.

Abhijit was placing trades from the couple's demat accounts

and huge brokerage payments ended up in the pockets of Doll Money. Of course, a percentage of that went to Abhijit as incentives. The NSE arbitration was vigilant enough to penalize the stockbroker with refunding all of the amount along with an 18 per cent interest per annum. The couple finally ended up getting almost double their portfolio value.

This is one curse of the stockbroking system you must be cautious of.

The best way for you to survive such a situation is to say no to the advisory being given to you for free. The other way is to accept the tips, analyse them on your own, and place only those trades that you feel may go right as per your own analysis. Of course, to do that you need to know some bits of technical or fundamental analysis yourself.

Hidden charges

This can be seen as a subset of the category mentioned above. But there are multiple layers here.

First, multiple tips are recommended to the trader through the day on a regular basis. For instance, traders are made to place option trades multiple times, with an entry and exit price every time. In such trades, a small percentage of profit is booked every time and the trader is told to place trades in volume. If your trading account is with a discount broker, then irrespective of the fact that your broker charges you brokerage at lot or order level, your trade will be placed at a single lot level only. This is done for the simple reason that every time you place a trade, a fixed brokerage amount reaches the broker's bank account.

On the other hand, if your broker is a full-service one who charges brokerage on a percentage basis, then the order quantity will be high so that a decent percentage of your premium turnover amount converts to brokerage. Remember, the person who is making you trade has a brokerage target.

Second, it's not just the brokerage. A lot of stockbrokers will (mis)guide you and tell you that they have an ultra-modern, high-tech, algo-based software that will give you automatic signals about market entries and exits. You don't need to depend on any advisor as humans can make mistakes. Instead, there is a software designed by tech people with 50 years of data in it that has captured all types of market movements, one that is made to make you rich. And of course it does not make any mistakes. But you have to follow everything it says.

Their selling pitch goes somewhat like this: 'Sir, this is a one-time expense. You will easily recover the cover in the next few days. I strongly suggest you buy it. The cost is only about ₹50,000 to ₹1 lakh, based on the broker and the client.'

Again, you need to be aware of such gimmicks.

Yes, there are a few good ones out there but absolutely nothing in the world can give you perfect returns or anything close to perfect. All these cases are very much prevalent in the stock market. You need to be cautious.

Trading app glitches

While this is not a fraud or a scam, this is a big concern mostly for bigger volume-based traders. Although the amount of loss is a relative thing, smaller traders tend to leave the market when this happens to them. For a professional trader, this comes as a loss consistently. In this, basically your trading app stops working.

Let's say you have a demat account with XYZ stockbroker and one fine morning, you are looking to exit your position at a profit. You are trying to sell but it's just not happening. An error message keeps popping up.

'Your connection is not established…'

'Runtime error 404…'

'Server Error.'

Whatever the message, it just does not allow you to exit your trade, which would have given you a profit just a little while back. You shut down the app. After two hours, you open the app and you find that the position which would have been booked at a 10 per cent profit has not been exited and shows a loss of 10 per cent instead.

What really happened? Was your order delayed? Was it placed but wasn't showing the right price? Or did something else happen?

The fact of the matter is: you lost money in a trade which seemed to be in a profit. You send an email to customer support. You wait. Then you get a standard response. If you lost big money as per your capital, you file a complaint to the higher-ups.

They will show you a clause mentioned in your demat account-opening form that says:

The client is aware that trading over the internet involves many uncertain factors and that complex hardware, software, systems, communication lines, peripherals, etc., are susceptible to interruptions and dislocations. The stockbroker and the exchange do not make any representation or warranty that the stockbroker's IBT (internet-based trading) service will be available to the client at all times without any interruption.

In most arbitrations, this is the first line of defence most stockbrokers put forward.

In January 2024, there were 16 such cases where the trading app of one broker or the other stopped working due to temporary outage. In December last year, this number was 15. This implies that this is a constant affair.

Does this mean you can't defend yourself?

Well, there is a small chance you can.

First, things need to be really specific. Lesser the number of people it impacts, the greater the chance of the broker accepting it. If it happens with everyone, most brokers just say, 'We can't refund everyone.' However, if only a few complaints arise, some reputed brokers agree to pay a partial amount of the overall loss borne by the client. Having said this, it also depends on the broker. There are a few who never agree to any resort and there are a few who agree to an extent.

As a trader, you must screen-record the glitch, comment on what is going on, explain the issue, take screenshots, send an email to the broker, follow up on it multiple times, record all the calls being made, stay polite in those calls, and then try and extract as much information as possible. All of this will be proof during arbitration.

It will test your patience but if you feel the amount is worth it, you must follow up.

Unauthorized trading/misusing client funds

Let's say you have a demat account and there is a possibility that you may or may not be in touch with any of the broker's representatives. If you are not in touch, great. But let's say you are and then you start seeing something going on in your trading accounts—positions being taken, money being lost or even made, but you have limited understanding of what's really going on.

What would you do?

Let me explain.

There was a client named Prashant Kumar (name changed) who had a demat account with a stockbroker named Fixed Broking (name changed). The client did not share his credentials with the stockbroker but somehow a sales executive started trading in Prashant's account. Furthermore, it was a big trading quantity. Prashant never gave any authorization or consent to said employee to place trades on his behalf. These unauthorized trades led to a loss of around ₹14.25 lakh. Apart from the trading loss, a brokerage in the range of ₹5.19 lakh was also generated.

Prashant approached SEBI and filed a complaint against the broker. The NSE set up a committee and the case was discussed. The broker gave their own version of the story. Eventually, the committee asked the broker to produce call recordings, email responses or WhatsApp chats as proof of trade authorization provided by the client.

However, Fixed Broking was not able to submit any such proof that would satisfy the NSE committee.

On the other hand, the client submitted everything he had in terms of written or oral communication with the stockbroker. Eventually, the client was awarded a decent compensation with a refund of the brokerage amount. Obviously, the whole loss amount was not returned but eventually the client received 70 per cent to 75 per cent of the overall loss incurred (in this case around ₹12 lakh).

This is the kind of fraud that is prevalent in the industry but people rarely get to know since they happen to a client and cases are sorted within panels and committees of the exchange as well as the regulator. Not many media houses report these stories either. However, as long as you have all proof, you can assume you are safe.

While highly unlikely, what if a SEBI-registered stockbroker defrauds you? Well, for every crook there are regulations and penalties on violations placed by SEBI. The regulator has made the system completely online and easy to follow. That's what the next chapter is about.

15

WHAT TO DO WHEN A BROKER DEFRAUDS YOU

Read this complaint that one of our subscribers had against a stockbroker:

Dear ADB team,

This is the story of my brother and me. On 28 May 2024 we made a profit of ₹20 lakh on our capital of ₹19 lakh. We were very happy. It was a gamble but it paid off.

The next day, our demat account with a bank-based stockbroker was sitting at a negative ₹1.5 lakh.

First, we thought it must be a glitch, so we checked our PnL statements and it showed a profit. When we reached out to customer support, they said there was a penalty of ₹42 lakh on our account. We asked why, to which they said they didn't know but would get back to us.

After continuous calls and posts, they said it was not a penalty but their account had been frozen. Again, we asked for the reason and they said they didn't know. So we waited. It's been a week now and they still have not released our funds.

We sold our home to invest in the stock market. My brother and I are devastated and it's taking a toll on our

> mental health. We begged the broker to at least give us our capital back if not the profit. They said they would tell me about this in some time. Can you please help us?

We receive such emails on a regular basis from users across stockbrokers. As discussed in another chapter earlier, this is a service-related complaint—that is, Type 1.

We called the victim, Ravi Shankar (name changed), and assisted him in filing complaints with the compliance officer of the broker, and then in the next few days on SEBI's SCORES portal and then at the Smart ODR.

Unfortunately, these things are normal in the stock market. So what do you do in case of extra brokerage, unauthorized trades, or an app glitch?

You would file a SEBI complaint.

But!

That can't be the starting point. In fact, that's the last resort. Otherwise, your complaints will just be rejected. You need to follow a chain of command starting from the broker.

The first point of contact must always be the broker's customer support. If you are sending an email, that's fine, but if you are making a call, record it. You will always find the contact details of the stockbroker on the Contact Us page of the website, in either the header or the footer.

Let's say you contacted your stockbroker but there was no response. Maybe you even sent a reminder, which did not change anything. Time to use you stockbroker's escalation matrix.

Some stockbrokers have this information on the 'contact us' page or as a separate escalations page. That's where you will find the email IDs and phone numbers of:

- Head of customer care
- Compliance officer

- CEO & MD

Let's understand who these people are.

The head of customer care, as the title suggests, is the head of the service or support team. The compliance officer is someone who takes care of compliance, regulations and the rules the regulator sets. This person looks at the customers, the broker itself, and the overall rules of the stock market. The CEO and/or MD is the top person. They take all the tough calls.

None of these people want the complaint to move to the next level, i.e. SEBI. This is because the head of customer care and the compliance officer know that if they fail to address the problem, their seniors and bosses would know they have done a bad job.

The CEO and/or MD would always want the customer to be happy for two reasons:

1. An unhappy customer will leave their services and open an account with a rival stockbroker. This will be a loss to them and a profit to the rival.
2. When such a complaint is raised with the regulator, this information becomes public to everyone including, but not limited to, competitors, SEBI and existing as well as potential clients. No business wants that to happen.

Now, let's say you have talked to all these levels and are still not happy with the solution.

It's then time to move out of the broker and complain to the big boss, SEBI.

You register yourself on SCORES (SEBI Complaints Redress System). This is a web portal where you can file a complaint against the stockbroker (or any stock market-regulated entity under SEBI).

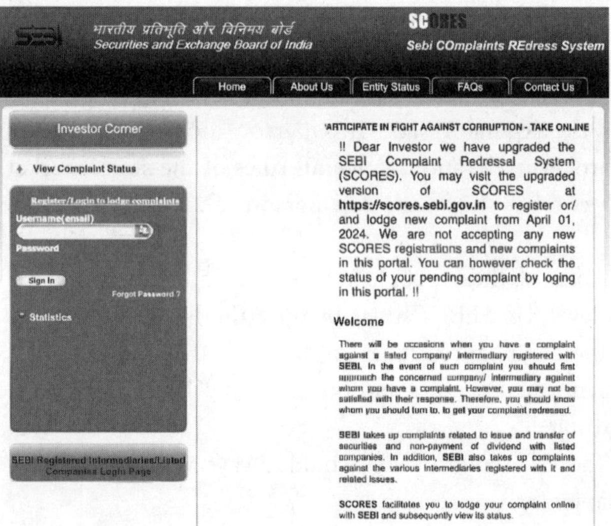

This was what it used to look like. But things have changed and this is what it looks like now:

Once you register and log in to the system, this is what you see:

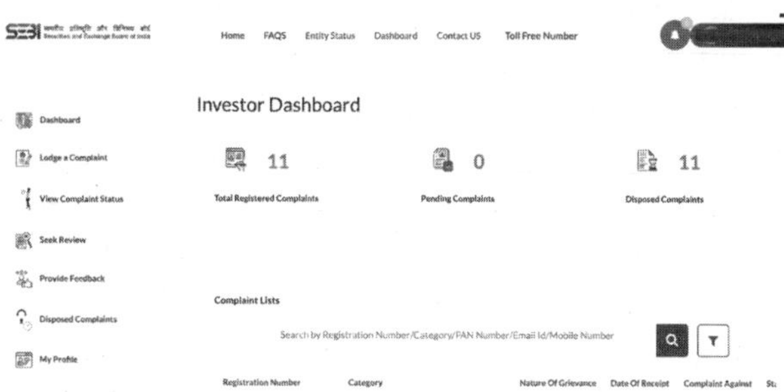

To file a complaint, you click on 'Lodge a Complaint'.

A new screen will show 29 blocks and you need to select 'stockbroker' (if the complaint is against any other entity, you make the corresponding choice).

That's when you reach the actual complaint form.

Let's go through all the fields one by one and understand what you need for each:

1. First is the 'Complaint Against'.
   Here you need to select the broker that you have the complaint against. Let's say you choose Divya Securities (this is only for reference purpose).

2. Next is 'Stock Exchange'.
   Here you need to pick the exchange you want SEBI to notify if they get to resolving this complaint.
   Let's say you picked the NSE.
3. Next is 'Client ID'.
   This is where you insert your client ID with the stockbroker you are complaining against. You can find this from your trading/web app or in your email with your account opening details.
4. Then there is 'DP ID'.
   This is the depository participant ID of your stockbroker. This information can be found on the broker's website or in your trading app.
5. Finally, you choose the complaint type out of the many displayed. We have already discussed these in a prior chapter. Depending on your issue, you choose an option. You are also allowed to choose more than one option. But remember, you need to provide a description for each of the options you choose.
   You can also upload any document, proof, screenshot, recording, etc., in the description of the complaint type chosen.
6. Then you click on 'Submit'. Once you do this, there will be a small confirmation pop-up to preview all the files uploaded. There will be a small 'Click here to preview' link along with the upload button. You need to click that and validate the image uploaded.
7. After that, just click 'Submit' and the complaint will be submitted successfully. The complaint will then be displayed in the 'View Complaint Status' section of the SCORES portal.

Now what?

Complaint Lists

Filter ▾ | Search by Registration Number/Category/PAN Number/Email Id/Mobile Number

Registration Number	Category	Nature Of Grievance	Date Of Receipt	Complaint Against	Status	Action
SEBIE/PB24/ROPA/004842/1	Stock Broker	Non-execution of order	03-05-2024		Pending	

This complaint will be redirected to the stockbroker—i.e. the compliance officer as well as the CEO/MD. There will be a few rounds of discussion, primarily responses from each side to the other. The regulator can choose to dispose of the complaint. However, you can take up this complaint to the next order of hierarchy at any given point in time. This is unlike how it was earlier, when you were forced to follow the hierarchy as is.

How do we know this?

If you click on the Arrow icon shown along with each of the complaints filed by you, you will see this pop-up window:

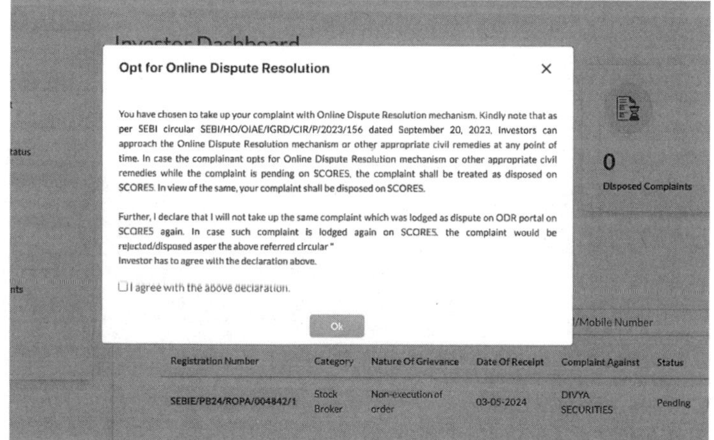

Basically, the point is simple. You tried complaining using the SCORES portal but ended up responding to the broker in a 'your word against mine' situation. That's what you want to get out of to file a dispute.

You can use the next level which is called ODR—Online Dispute Resolution, aka SMART ODR. As written in the pop-up above, it says you are allowed to move to the next level but then you can't come back to the SCORES portal. Even if you do come back and file the same complaint, it will be automatically disposed of.

You need to understand one thing: SCORES is managed by SEBI and Smart ODR is operationally handled by the NSE and related exchanges. It is a mechanism by SEBI that allows it to cut itself off from the operational headaches of running the service or handling complaints.

So how is the complaint handled from here?

First, as soon as you opt for the Smart ODR, your existing SCORES complaint stands disposed of, as shown here:

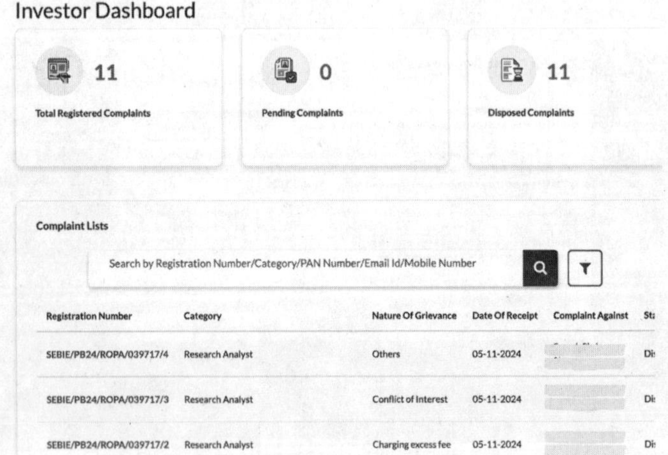

Moving on from SCORES implies you were not happy with the outcome or the resolution received.

You move to Smart ODR with this link: https://smartodr.in/login.

You need to register again. Once that is done, this is what you see:

This clearly shows you the required process.

So, let's file a dispute against the same entity. If you click on 'File a New Dispute', the portal will ask you this:

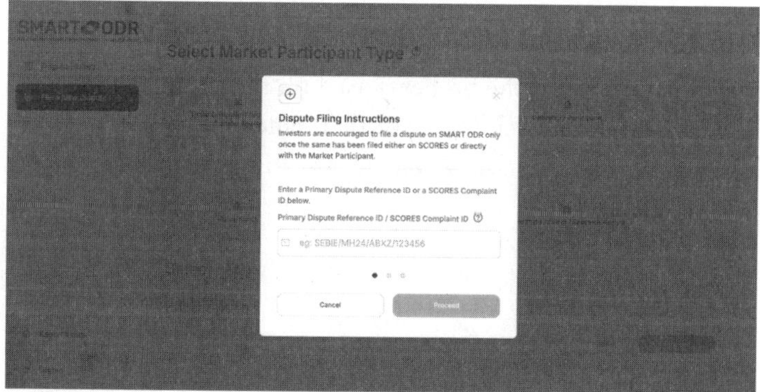

If you choose 'Yes' here, it will ask you:

- Date of lodging primary dispute—i.e., when did you file the complaint for the first time
- Dispute reference number (you can use the SCORES portal complaint reference number)

However, if you choose 'No', it will not allow you to file the dispute and ask you to first file an initial complaint with the entity directly. This is what we discussed earlier in this chapter.

After entering yes, this is what we see:

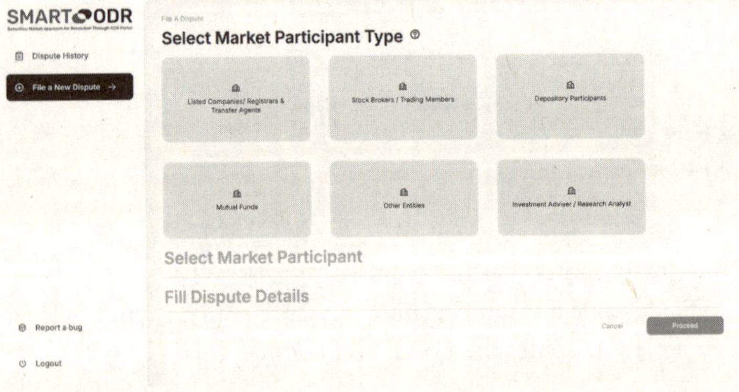

You simply have to pick the 'Brokers' block, since we are filing a complaint against the broker. Based on the complaint, it could be any of the other entities. We then enter the required details again. This is nothing different from most of what we entered in the SCORES portal.

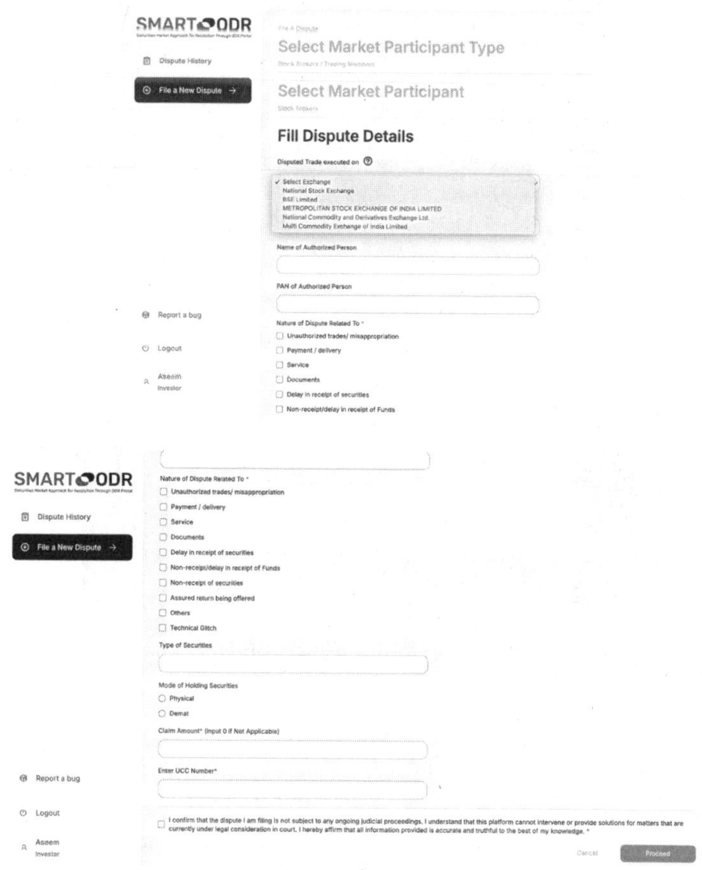

After entering all these details, it's time to 'Proceed'. Once you click on that button, it will again ask you for confirmation in the form of a pop-up.

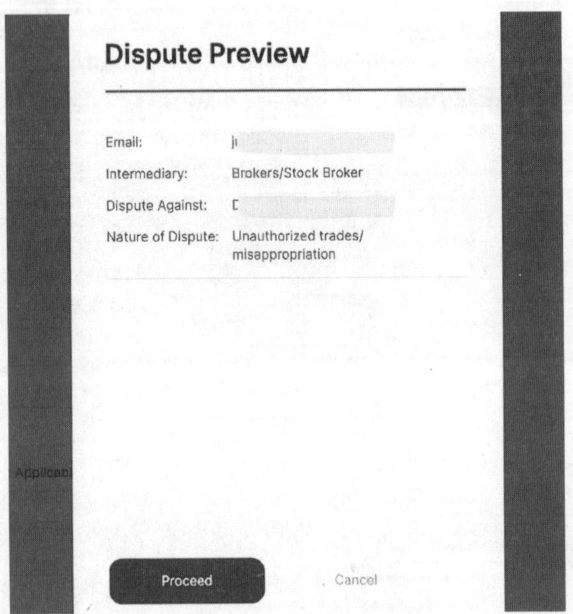

If you select 'Proceed', it will successfully file your dispute in the portal.

The intermediary or the registered entity then gets 21 days to respond to what has been filed against them. Assuming all the details you have entered are correct, your dispute will be communicated or else it will be disposed of. Once you get a response, there are two possibilities: the complaint gets disposed of after a solution or an apt response by the intermediary or you may be needed to respond to the answer provided.

If there is no solution, the exchange sets up a GRC (Grievance Redressal Committee) in which representatives from your end and the broker's end will be invited for a discussion over Google Meet or Zoom. Both parties are given an equal opportunity to air their views. The parties also need to bring all their proof.

There will be a moderator from the exchange along with an

advisor appointed by the exchange who comes with experience of the capital market and can be deemed as a neutral party. There will be an attempt in this meeting for a mutual resolution. The advisor may choose to declare an outcome with a penalty for either of the parties as per what the book says. The party that is not satisfied with the outcome of this meeting may choose to escalate it to the next level, which is arbitration.

There is a panel that sits in this arbitration and both sides are heard again in depth. Both sides are required to provide proof on their complaints and comments. If any of the sides needs time, they can request for a few days.

In this step, there is a possibility that the arbitration panel may choose to go ahead with what the GRC committee had decided or they may choose to reverse the division. All the steps are documented and the final outcome is first declared to both the parties and then is released on the NSE website.

If you are still not happy with the resolution being offered, you can challenge this order as well. There is something called SAT, Securities Appellate Tribunal. Here is its technical definition:

The Securities Appellate Tribunal is a statutory body established under the provisions of Section 15K of the Securities and Exchange Board of India Act, 1992, to hear and dispose of appeals against orders passed by the Securities and Exchange Board of India or by an adjudicating officer under the Act.

The most important thing is that the orders passed by SEBI or any adjudication officer can be challenged. You get 45 days to do so. If the SAT finds sufficient reason for a delay in the appeal, that can be condoned. The SAT, after hearing the case, may pass an order or remit the matter back to SEBI for further consideration.

And what if your expectations were not met by the SAT?

A SAT order can be challenged in the Supreme Court within

the next 60 days. This then becomes a chain of command that started from a broker's customer executive and ends with the Supreme Court of India.

However, very few cases reach this point. Most are solved earlier in the process.

Now that you have an idea about the complaint redressal mechanism, are you safe?

Mostly yes. But there are always loopholes. Read on to know more.

Part 5

STOCK-MARKET EDUCATION SCAMS

16

OFFLINE CLASSES SCAM

Do people always get defrauded online when it comes to the stock market? Of course not. It may happen offline too. Remember, scammers scam people in the name of the stock market. It's not really the stock market that's looting people.

Let me take you to Hisar, a mid-sized town in Haryana.

A new stock market trainer launched his institute in one of the poshest localities.

Host: 'You said anyone can be a millionaire by investing ₹20,000. How is that possible?'

This host was a local who hosted a town-based YouTube channel. The guest named Sanjay was someone who was claiming he can make everyone a trader with his 'protocol'-based trading.

Sanjay: 'Thank you, *Sirji*, for coming to our institute and spreading real awareness about the stock market. A lot of people have gone bankrupt in the trading world but there is nothing that trading has done wrong to them. It's the people who end up harming themselves. There is a song in a Bollywood movie "Munni Badnaam hui"; similarly, people have made the phrase "trading badnaam".'

Host: 'True, can bankrupt people still make a comeback and earn money?'

Sanjay: 'Of course. You might have seen and heard of a lot of businessmen going bankrupt but they do make a comeback.

Here, when we teach you about the stock market, we can tell whether you will end up bankrupt or not, just by talking to you.'

Host: 'And how do you figure that out?'

Sanjay: 'Today anybody and everybody opens a demat account and thinks that they are a trader. All they have to do is buy a call or a put based on market movement. For me, those people are nothing less than gamblers.'

Host: 'Yes, a lot of people in our small towns call trading gambling.'

Sanjay: 'Is there any business in the world that can make you money without you knowing anything about it?'

This went on for a while.

Till here, the story seems to be genuine. You will probably say Sanjay is right in his observations and seems to be a very wise stock market trainer. But hold on.

Host: 'Okay, what do you teach that makes you think yours is a complete course or curriculum?'

Sanjay: 'There are a few rules one needs to follow. I can guarantee and challenge the whole country or even the world that you won't face a loss. If you do, we are here!'

What happened here? Do you still believe in Sanjay?

Here is what happened once people heard and read about Sanjay's tall claims. About 500 people from that mid-sized town enrolled in his course, each paying a fee of ₹20,000. That's a revenue of ₹1 crore. Sanjay taught for about seven to eight days. After that he left the town, saying some of his business partners had defrauded him.

Later, Sanjay came back online and said, 'Friends, my business partners backstabbed me. So I have come to my hometown in Haryana. I have decided to teach the stock market to a new batch. If you have already paid for the course, you can come here. This is my address.'

About 200 more people from his hometown enrolled with the same fee. This time he taught only for one day and then did something no one can even imagine.

He faked a SEBI raid. When students reached the institute, they were greeted by someone standing outside the building.

'I am from SEBI and we have conducted a raid here. There were complaints against this institute and I have been given special orders from the PMO (Prime Minister's Office). The local DSP has been called, Mr Sanjay is in our custody and he will be interrogated,' he said to everyone who turned up.

'We will also be checking if students were involved in the scam. If that is true, they will also be arrested,' the person said sternly.

Listening to this, most students fled. No one wanted any trouble.

However, it's likely that this fake SEBI raid was really planned by Sanjay. A few days later, these very SEBI officials tried to extort another institute in the city but were caught by the actual police.

Sanjay is still untraceable.

Unfortunately, this filmy story is entirely real. There has been no local reporting, no media discussions, nothing online, and no police investigations against Sanjay. All that's left are the silent cries of the 500–700 people who lost money. These people were not gullible students or youngsters. They were a mix of all age groups, genders, professional and educational backgrounds. This is just one case. There are many.

We investigated a case where a New Delhi-based finfluencer on Instagram was involved. One of our team members travelled and stayed in their offline batch.

The influencer would come on Instagram and say extreme things such as:

Leave your 9-to-5 job. Why crib under a boss all your life. Come trade with me and I will help you become a full-time trader.

I can guarantee that anyone and everyone can be a trader. All you need is to trust me and take my offline classes.

I challenge so-called traders out there. Come and show profits like I do; I know you won't be able to.

I have said this repeatedly—if someone makes extreme or unrealistic statements, it should be obvious they are not legit.

I have seen hundreds of people flocking from different parts of the country to these offline batches to stay in mediocre-quality PG rooms and learning nothing new. What is being taught can be learnt online or for free on YouTube. So, what exactly is happening in these unreal classes?

Setups!

Every trader, whether they have been trading for six months or six years, has a trading setup. This is basically a zone in the market based on a few conditions of stock-market technical analysis that gives out an entry price and an exit price (at both target and stop-loss levels).

This particular social media influencer calling people to his location to learn about the stock market from him was charging ₹18,000 for a 20-day course. More than 500 people were participating, with around 100 of them paying an additional ₹10,000 for accommodation. After the 20 days, most felt cheated but kept their feelings inside.

The worst part is that these offline cases end up being limited to towns and cities. They don't get visibility with a wider audience. Thus, the same scamster can try the trick over and over again in a new place. Having said this, I am not saying offline coaching or classes are wrong.

In fact, this is one of the best ways to learn trading since your tutor is right in front of you and you can ask all kinds of questions. At the same time, you need to be wary of people who are trying to lure you.

First, persuasion is easy in the stock market. Most people don't have the skills to trade and very few are able to make a regular profit. So, when someone claims they have something that is exclusive and rare, people want to believe it to be true.

Second, don't fall for tall claims and profit screenshots.

Third, look for trainers who position themselves as educators and not dream sellers. The right ones will keep your expectations directed towards learning. If you ask them whether they will assist you in trading in the stock market, the genuine ones will negate that demand.

How do you know that the offline institute has genuine intentions? A few conclusions:

- They won't lure you or show any sort of profit screenshots.
- They will promise you learning only and give no assurance of what is going to happen monetarily to your profits after the course.
- They will be open to smaller batches of even four to five students, in comparison to what happens in the online space.
- They won't arrange huge seminars/workshops of 200–300 students with an agenda of making everyone a trader. No one can teach these many students.
- No live trading will be promised in such batches.
- Doubt-clearing sessions will generally be arranged regarding your setup.
- Proper conceptual and practical knowledge will be shared.

By the way, there is an even bigger animal in this space. The lord of stock market classes—let's welcome ourselves to the world of offline workshops. What happens in such workshops? That's what we will find out next.

17

REALITY BEHIND EXPENSIVE STOCK MARKET WORKSHOPS

'This is where we are going to place the stop loss,' the founder of an option-chain-based analytics software said. His one-hour session was part of a three-day workshop at a resort in Bangalore.

Suddenly the market started seeing a dip.

'Okay, I think this is a sudden move. Maybe it will dip a bit more. Let me quickly change the stop-loss level,' the same founder said. And just like that, he rests his stop-loss price 200 points below the earlier one.

'Didn't he just say to not change the stop-loss level, and that one must follow what his software tells us to do?' I overheard someone saying.

'Wait, let me take the stop-loss even further. *Risk hai to ishq hai*, huh!' the founder smirked.

'I am not buying his software for sure. What's the point if he is using his discretion like that?' the guy behind me said.

In the next few minutes, the software founder booked a loss of ₹5.5 lakh, which could have easily been an exit loss of ₹33,000. There seemed to be no discipline in his trades. The guy behind me would have lost much less money on that trade because this poor chap, like many others in the banquet hall, was just copying the trade being made on the stage.

While the online space is full of fishy business, offline workshops are a whole other beast.

For example, there is a workshop where you are told you will be 'taught' complex stock market concepts face to face. Now, add the fact that you will live in a luxurious five-star resort for two–three days. Then mix a few social media finfluencers to this cocktail.

Once the event starts, the ones who pay can go ahead and talk to the celebrity finfluencers during lunch or otherwise. How much is the payment for such an event, you may ask? There is a range that varies from ₹70,000 to ₹1.5 lakh, depending on the location, kind of guests coming in, scale of the event, and so on.

What happens here? Do people who pay see a transformation in their trading or investing? Do all of them start making money magically?

Education, learning, conceptual and practical understanding of trading do happen. There are also inspirational stories that act as a huge motivating factor for the guests.

However, apart from the meals, education, on-stage discussions, stories and influencer selfies, there are sessions where you can open your laptops, log in to your trading accounts, listen carefully to what the star on the stage is saying (and doing) with his live trades, and just copy those with your capital.

No one from the event management team tells people to do this. But this is pretty much the reason guests pay so much for these events. It is not irrational to think that the paid guest would want to make some returns on the money spent.

While there are genuine speakers, what's the fun in that?

Yet, if someone is trading in the live market in these workshops and you follow along, it's not just illegal but also senseless.

Going back to the story of the startup founder who booked a

huge loss in front of everyone, there's more. After everything, he still had the guts to smile and say, 'Well, this is the stock market. This happens all the time. All that matters is how you make a comeback.' He did not take any sessions for the rest of the day.

The whole room clapped, most likely because they had no other choice. Almost everyone who copied his trade ended up losing money. This is not the only reason for not attending such events. All this happens without any authorization, certification or SEBI licence. The audience is simply made to believe that whatever is happening is right.

Yes, there is education and inspiration, but it's nothing that you can't get online or from a book.

Let's say you still make some kind of profit. Maybe you make double of what you paid for. But can you replicate this once the workshop is done? Can you repeat everything on your own once you are home? Even if you spend six months using all the learnings you got, do you think you can become a successful and profitable trader just by attending such an event? Apart from socializing, does this make sense?

It doesn't really.

You should go for such events if: a) there is no entry fee and you are looking to have a fan moment only, b) you are not trading based on what guests are saying, even if they are SEBI-registered (which is also illegal), and c) you just want to experience such an event. If you are looking for a get-rich scheme through a two-day interaction with a person whom you are actually meeting for the first time, stay at home.

In the next chapter, I will take you to the bigger industry of stock market education.

18

ARE ALL STOCK MARKET COURSES A SCAM?

No. Education is one of the most important pillars of the stock market and genuine teaching must only prosper.

This chapter talks about the other side.

'Hey guys, you know me. I have been trading in the stock market for the last 15 years. Do you want to learn how I can help you make money from the stock market? I will be giving a webinar this Saturday. Do join, only for ₹99,' a known stock market YouTuber Vishal Nalkhan (name changed) said in one of his videos. He also runs ads on Facebook and Instagram for the same webinar.

One day, I also thought I would join to see what exactly it's all about. The webinar ran for one hour. There were zero stock market concepts taught. The one hour covered:

- Why is stock market learning important?
- Why does learning the stock market from him make 100 per cent sense?
- How did he win a US-based investing championship award?
- How can he make everybody a trader?
- Why is everyone who has not taken his course missing out on making it big in their lives?

In other words, there was not a single minute of stock market education in the one hour for which hundreds of users paid ₹99 each. It was just a one-hour pitch for his course that was worth ₹10,000. For the duration of the webinar, he kept showing a QR code through which the course would be priced at ₹6,999 instead. 'It is a limited-time offer. So scan this QR code and grab this exclusive discount on this super amazing course,' he went on.

The QR code worked at a discounted price of ₹6,999 even three months after the webinar. Later, we researched a bit more about his course and were surprised to find some nasty details. This ₹6,999 course pitched his ₹70,000 course, which was an offline workshop for a few days in a five-star hotel. I would have loved to take part in that workshop, but there was a possibility of being recognized by some people, and that might not have been pleasant.

More than 20 users complained to us through our YouTube channel about this person. Some of them had attended the ₹70,000 programme. They said there was live market trading, analysis, and then pitching of his ₹10 lakh-worth course.

A few people did sign up for the ₹10 lakh programme. This was very private and we don't know what happens there.

In a sense, this whole course thing is basically a sales funnel where the only thing that is happening is 'upselling' to the next course.

'Never mind, let's investigate what's really going on,' I thought.

My brother is a chartered accountant and runs a firm in a different city. I called him up.

'*Bhai*, can we get the financial statements of a private limited company?'

'Of course you can. From the MCA website,' my brother said.

'Okay. I am sending you the name of the companies on WhatsApp. I need the balance sheets, PnL and cash-flow statements of these firms for the last six years,' I said.

'But why?' he asked.

'For research. Also, I want your analysis about the entity's financial situation when it comes to stock market trading and investments,' I said.

A few days later, brother called me at 11.30 p.m. and said, 'He is at a loss of ₹3.5 crore! You told me he is a stock market educator. How is he teaching without making money?'

'That's exactly what I wanted to know!' I responded.

'But how is this possible? Are his students okay with this? Isn't this ethically wrong on this Nalkhan guy's part? I mean, I wouldn't teach CA students if I could not clear the exam myself,' my asked.

'I am pretty sure no one knows that he has been losing money. In fact, I have heard that he does some yearly PnL videos and claims that he is profitable. I think such people don't really have any ethics or shame. They are in the game only for money. I had my doubts when I saw him upselling all his courses,' I tried to explain.

'Well, that is a bit disappointing. Good night.'

'Good night!'

The next day, I told my team we would be making a video on this. It was shot, edited and published. Till date, more than 500,000 people have seen that video and hopefully a decent percentage of them understood the intent behind trainings like these.

I must repeat that I am not saying stock market training is a scam. It's a noble profession if done right. For that matter, I also run an app named Stock Pathshala that focuses on stock market live classes and batches.

When it comes to stock market education, we know that

there is no formal degree or diploma in our country. It's not in any curriculum. So, if one wants to really learn about the stock market, there are books, and now with the advent of social media, there are a lot of YouTube channels that are trying to fill the gap. Then, there are local businesses that run stock market courses.

Here are some fancy lines that are used by those who are misleading in the name of courses:

- *Come, join my course. You will be made part of our Telegram channel and I will share daily levels with stop-loss and target price.* This is basically a SEBI-unregistered research analyst who is trying to lure people towards tips.
- *If you join my stock market course, I will help you increase your profits. There will be an onboarding fee and then a cut from the profit made.* In other words, a profit-sharing scheme, which is also illegal.
- *I have made so much money from the stock market. Check out my car, my house, oh, sorry, the cash just dropped. Once you pay ₹5,000 per month, I will share strategies with you that can give you assured 20 per cent daily returns.*

Obviously, buying these courses does not generally end well for the retail trader/investor. They end up saying, 'That course was just a scam. I paid ₹20,000 and got nothing.' This creates a difficult situation for everyone.

For the ones who are really offering the 'education' part in courses, when approaching their client or vice versa, one of two things happen:

- The client shows no interest due to an enigma created in the stock market universe about courses, as mentioned earlier.

- The client still expects the course provider to offer tips and other fancy stuff that such courses are generally known for.

So, is anyone really interested in learning?

Let's first define stock market education in black-and-white terms. Education means learning the concepts within different aspects of the stock market.

- How do you find support and resistance in a trending market? This is education.
- How does the option chain help you get an idea about the option contract's volumes and trends? This is also education.
- How does the PE ratio help you perform a quick competitive analysis of different companies in a specific industry? Again, education.

But!

- How will TATA Motors' share price definitely reach a level of 1,100 tomorrow morning? This is NOT education.

Let me reiterate the difference between scams and courses. If someone is trying to show you dreams of a lavish lifestyle or financial freedom in one or two years, RUN. If they say they have reached a point where they can share their success with you, having come from a humble background, and they just want others to make the best of their time and money, RUN.

Stock market courses with an expectation of learning concepts is genuine. But it must be genuine from both sides. If you want the tutor or trainer to teach you honestly, then you must also keep honest expectations. You should go into it to learn the concepts and then apply them practically, subsequently seeking clarity from the trainer. Learn how to catch a fish, and in this case, don't expect the tutor to serve you the fish on a platter.

People who teach generally have a decent educational background or a wide range of experience in trading and/or investing (in terms of number of years and/or experience of trading in more than one segment). In today's world of too many scams, you should ask for an NISM (National Institute of Securities Markets) certification in the field of trading that the trainer is teaching.

NISM is an educational initiative by SEBI aimed at enhancing knowledge and professional standards in the Indian securities markets. It offers various certification programmes around financial services, stock market operations, research and investment advisory.

Some of the key basic-level certifications being offered include:

- NISM Series I: Currency Derivatives Certification
- NISM Series V-A: Mutual Fund Distributors Certification
- NISM Series VIII: Equity Derivatives Certification
- NISM Series X-A & X-B: Investment Adviser Certifications
- NISM Series XII: Securities Markets Foundation Certification

These not only serve as regulatory requirements but also help individuals gain a deeper understanding of financial markets, making them well-equipped for various roles in the industry.

It also helps if the person is a SEBI-registered IA or RA.

A proper trainer will explain to you a) the concepts and modules to be taught, b) the basic objective of the course, c) the expectations a student must keep, d) the duration, e) the number of classes/workshops, and f) their background.

A scamster trainer will tell you a) the amount of money he/she made from his/her strategy, b) the money you can start expecting from trading after the course, c) the dreams you can have during the day, d) shortcut methods of making money from the stock market that people don't know, and e) other weird things.

Interestingly, former SEBI chairperson Madhabi Puri Buch had said she respected the education part within social media influencers. It's just the ones who showed dreams to gullible traders and investors she had a problem with.

An actual stock market course will come with a plan and a curriculum.

Always remember:

- You will find specific classes/chapters with topic names.
- There will be multiple doubt-clearing sessions.
- There will be practical workshops.
- There will be an expectation set by the course-provider about the learnings.
- Every class will have assignments and study material.
- None of the SEBI regulations will be violated during the pitching and while the course is running.
- The best one will have an examination and issue a proper certificate at the end.

You won't feel cheated during and after taking such a course (assuming your own expectation was to learn). Stock market courses are not a scam as long as you have done due diligence on the concepts being taught, the objectives being specified, and the background of the trainer. It also requires that you have a clear intent of learning.

19

THE GLAMOUR OF PONZI SCHEMES

'A*rey* Sharma ji, I am telling you. These people are very trustworthy, otherwise who in today's world gives you a 15 per cent monthly return? I have been getting it for the last five months. To top that, remember I told you about that trip? They were the ones who arranged this trip for me and your *bhabhi* ji.'

'But Arora ji, in my whole life I have not seen anyone giving such returns every month. Eight per cent to 10 per cent? By the way, how many people have invested in this scheme?' Satish Sharma asked with a mix of caution and curiosity.

'325, Sharma ji. When I joined three months back, there were only 80 people. Do you remember Vijay Gupta whom we met in the club? He suggested that I join this investment plan. He had joined about six months back and is on a Europe trip these days,' Arora said exuberantly.

'Really? Which country? I am sure he went to Amsterdam, Arora ji!' Sharma said cheekily.

'Ha ha!' Arora laughed.

The next day at 11 a.m. sharp, both Sharma and Arora were sitting at the reception of Creditbulls Investments Private Limited. Arora was going to be a referrer for Sharma in the pyramid plan.

'Arora ji, please come. Let's talk in the conference room,' Prerna, a senior sales manager at Creditbulls, said.

Then the presentation for Sharma started.

'Arora ji, how was your Dubai trip and the five-star-resort stay?' Prerna asked

'Very good, Prerna ji. Thanks for the hospitality,' Mr. Sharma responded with folded hands.

'No problem, sir. It's our duty to keep our investors happy. Your trust in us keeps us moving to work even harder for you,' Prerna said.

'So, Mr Sharma, welcome to Creditbulls Investments. I am Prerna Wadhera, a senior investment advisor. We are an investment company in the business since 1989 and we have been investing in the equity, commodities and real estate markets for the last 35 years. We are a government-approved organization. You can see the GSTIN and company registration information here in this slide,' Prerna continued.

'Our focus is one thing—getting the highest returns for our national and international clients who have funds but don't have knowledge about investing in the right place,' Prerna went on.

The rest of the presentation highlighted the returns and value Creditbulls Investments had brought to its clients.

'How do I feel safe about my money? I am a retired employee and have my provident fund savings with me. I find stock market investments too risky,' Sharma expressed his concern.

'You are absolutely right, sir. There is no doubt that investment in the stock market is a bit risky since the market can go in any direction. You seem to be a very intelligent and aware person, Mr Sharma.

'However, like I said, we have been trading for 35 years, so we know the market cycles and understand which industries perform during what time of the year. Plus, our researchers are very experienced. Every researcher has a monthly salary of ₹10 lakh. Now you can imagine how serious Creditbulls must be when it comes to investments,' Prerna explained.

She must have said these lines many times in her career.

Sharma looked at Arora, who was smiling.

'Okay, ma'am. What are the different plans you have?' he asked.

'We have three plans for investments. Here are the details:

1. Monthly ₹1 lakh investment, get 2 per cent returns; no lock-in
2. Monthly ₹3 lakh investment, get 5 per cent returns; lock-in of 1 year
3. Monthly ₹5 lakh investment, get 10 per cent returns; lock-in of 2 years

'The more you invest in us, the more returns you get,' Prerna clarified.

'But Arora ji is getting monthly returns of 15 per cent?' Sharma asked.

'Yes, he is. That is because he upgraded himself to an Exclusive Diamond Plan. For that, there is an upfront file charge of ₹5 lakh with a monthly investment of ₹10 lakh and lock-in of 5 years. You can also start with that plan. You will get one international and two domestic holidays as well that you can enjoy with family, or friends,' she explained.

'Okay, I think we can go with this plan,' Sharma said confidently. Arora reacted with surprise.

'*Wah* Sharma ji. Good choice. We will go together on the next holiday. Prerna ji, can you arrange that?'

'Absolutely,' Prerna assured. 'I will send the plan and payment details to your email and WhatsApp number. You can make the necessary payments and share the details. Welcome to the

Creditbulls Investments family, Mr Sharma.'

Prerna had conducted more than a hundred such meetings in the last three months and closed 70 of them. Most of these meetings were arranged based on references from existing investors. She did not have to call clients anymore, like at her first job where she was making 100 calls a day to get demat accounts opened and get them to trade with a SEBI-registered broker. Her salary with that broker was ₹15,000 plus incentives, totalling to about ₹20,000. Here, in the last three months, she had made a total of ₹2 lakh already.

There were five other 'senior investment advisors' like Prerna. The other advisors also had a background of handling customers in the finance space, with experience of three to four years. Meetings like these continued for another five months.

'Prerna ji, Vishal sir is not answering my call. He said he would be travelling but it's been five days. Today is 3 March and none of the investors have gotten their returns for the last month.' This was Chinmay, a service head with Creditbulls Investments. He seemed worried.

'Okay, that generally does not happen. Let me check with Vishal and Sanchit sir. They must be somewhere with network issues. Don't worry, and you can tell the investors not to worry,' Prerna said reassuringly.

'Alright, please confirm once you hear from them.'

'Of course, Chinmay.'

Prerna tried calling all day but the numbers were not connecting. The alternate numbers were also switched off.

'Prerna, did you get your salary this month?' Chinmay asked. It was 9 March.

'No,' she said.

'No one has,' Chinmay clarified.

A few days passed.

'Prerna ji, I did not get the deposit this month. I called the service team but they said there was some technical issue. Can you please check and confirm? Also, my holiday is scheduled for this month, right?' Sharma asked Prerna, who was not in the office.

'I will check, sir,' she responded.

Days and weeks passed and the next month arrived. The service team had stopped answering calls. Other team members were also not coming to the office. No one knew what was going on. The residences of both founders, Vishal Ghai and Sanchit Patel, were locked.

'Are they alright? I hope there has been no mishap,' Prerna said to Chinmay.

'Prerna, I have something to tell you. I have a friend at HDDF Bank. I gave him all the company account numbers that we share with the investors for monthly deposits. My friend had a look at these accounts and all of them were empty. There is no money there. All the money was transferred on 25 February to some other account,' Chinmay confided.

'Meaning?' Prerna asked.

'Meaning all our investors' money is gone. They have been looted. Vishal and Sanchit are frauds but no one knows,' Chinmay said.

The conversation died there.

In the meantime, investors had filed complaints with the local police station against Creditbulls Investments. The details they had around the GSTIN and company registration were all fake. The phone numbers on the website were not working. The website had stopped operating. There were no employees to get in touch with. Arora had ₹75 lakh stuck, while Sharma had given away around ₹50 lakh for investments. A total of around ₹200 crore was stuck. No one knew where the money was.

The local police kept saying, 'We are investigating the Ponzi scam case with the help of the cyber police. A case of IPC 420 has been filed against Vishal Ghai and Sanchit Patel. A case of abetting has also been filed against 10 employees of Creditbulls Investment. We have made three arrests including of Mr Ramesh, Ms Prerna and Mr Amit. They will be brought to the court this week for their next hearing.' This happened for another two years and nothing much moved. Vishal Ghai and Sanchit Patel's last location was London but before that they were in Dubai and Morocco, as per police investigations.

Ponzi Scam

What exactly is a Ponzi scam?

This is a kind of scam where money is taken from investors with an assurance of guaranteed timely returns. The scammer shows that the investments happen in the most exclusive financial products but the reality is different. People who invest in these schemes pay a capital for their returns. This capital is used to provide money to existing investors and they get told that these are the returns you have made from your investments. Then, new investors are acquired. The investment from these new investors is then used to pay the investors who joined earlier than them. This keeps on going as long as the scheme gets new investors regularly.

However, at any given point, if the new capital starts drying up, there won't be enough money to pay as returns to existing investors. This becomes a sign for the scammers who started the Ponzi scheme to run away with all the money that they have.

The term 'Ponzi' was derived from Charles Ponzi, who was the first scammer to have pulled off this sort of a scam.

Charles Ponzi

These scams are prevalent in India, especially in tier two, three and four cities and towns. The modus operandi in such cases is very similar to the one narrated in the story above.

Target 'Audience'

Retirees with a decent amount of money and with a limited understanding of technology and/or the financial market are the easiest targets. At the same time, the people who invest are given incentives to bring in more people—international holidays, gifts, event invites, and sometimes a percentage-based cut on the amount of new money brought in for investments.

The scammers create companies that are not registered with SEBI. The reason for this is that no such registration is possible. This format of investment is called CIS or Collective Investment

Scheme under SEBI Regulations, 1999. There are very limited companies and groups that have been allowed by the regulator. If you want to validate whether the CIS in your town is registered with SEBI or not, ask them their registration number and request them to show it on SEBI's official website.

All such schemes can be checked on the SEBI website page:

Moreover, as I have said before, under no condition can an entity or individual promise you guaranteed or assured returns of any kind. There are strict guidelines against saying such words, even in marketing. So, if some representative is telling you this with confidence or assurance, that is a strong sign for you to run in the opposite direction.

You also need to understand the whole agenda. There are no investments happening with the capital being infused by investors. It's just that money is being taken from one pocket and put into another. The scammer makes the most money.

As far as paid luxury holidays are concerned, if someone has paid ₹50 lakh to ₹60 lakh or more, it's easy to fund a vacation that may even cost ₹10 lakh. It's his or her own money. And in six months with ₹60 lakh of investments, 15 per cent return in total is in the range of ₹9 lakh–₹10 lakh.

Where is the rest of the money?

In bank accounts that are going to be zeroed out in a few weeks or months.

These kinds of scams happen in the name of the stock market but there is no involvement of the stock market at all because no trading or investing is happening. It's a mechanism for luring people in, as people believe that the stock market can give exuberant returns. It can, but not like this.

In India, the recent past has seen multiple Ponzi schemes being operated by various entities. Most of the scammers leave the country once found out. For instance, the founder of Creditbulls, Dhaval Solani, is sitting in Dubai at the time of writing this. Such scammers, even if found, take too long to be caught. The money recovery process is another challenge altogether.

So, next time you hear a relative vouching for such a scheme, tell the person to EXIT.

In the last chapter of this book, we will talk about the *Laxman rekha* of SEBI. What it can do, will do, or what it can't or won't do when you are stuck in some sort of fraud or scam.

Part 6

SEBI'S FINE LINE

20

SEBI HAS LIMITATIONS TOO

This chapter is a reality check for people who carelessly lose their money in get-rich-quick schemes or hand over their money to people on the internet or around them.

The stock market can be a place to get a decent return on your investments, but you must be aware about where the investments are being made—which companies, which mutual funds, bonds or schemes, and what the respective backgrounds of these entities are.

While no one expects you to be aware of price action strategies or anything technical, you need to do a background check of stock market entities—just like you would for a bank for a fixed deposit or a property that you want to invest in, or even a jewellery shop you want to buy a gold ring from.

Let me share a story with you.

This was three years back. It was a Friday morning in October. A notification popped up on my phone.

I had received an email from SEBI, which read something like this:

> This is with reference to the trailing mail.
>
> Please lodge your complaint on SEBI Complaints Redress System (SCORES) at https://www.scores.gov.in.
>
> Please note that as per circular No. SEBI/HO/OIAE/IGRD/CIR/P/2018/58 dated 26 March 2018, investors who wish to lodge a complaint are required to register themselves

on SCORES before lodging the complaint against a listed company, a SEBI-registered intermediary or a SEBI-recognized Market Infrastructure Institution. While registering the complaints, mandatory details like Name of the investor, Address, PAN, Mobile Number and E-mail ID are to be mandatorily provided for registration.

With Regards
Office of Investor Assistance and Education
SEBI

This was a response to a complaint I had filed against an unregistered tip-advisor at scores@sebi.gov.in.

This is the standard response you will always get after sending that email. The email expected me to file the complaint at the SEBI portal SCORES. All complaints against any SEBI-regulated entity are supposed to be filed at this portal. I was aware about this but this complaint was against an unregistered entity. Even if I attempted to file a complaint at SCORES against this unregistered entity, I wouldn't be able to. The SCORES portal only displays the entities that are registered with SEBI.

So, how can one really get the concern resolved?

Let's take a step back.

Oh, you have been defrauded. Well, sorry about that!

Now even if you email the SEBI ID, the regulator won't respond or it will send a template-based response as mentioned at the start of this chapter, since the entity does not fall under SEBI's regulations directly or is not violating any of its guidelines.

What option do you have then? The police?

Well, it can be excruciating but that seems to be the only option. That will then be followed by you filing a court case against the entity. In other words, SEBI unfortunately won't get involved.

When subjected to a fraudulent or an unpleasant experience in the stock market, many people don't even know what to do. A few look to file a complaint with SEBI but most don't really know whether the complaint will be handled or not.

To simplify this, let's list the type of complaints one may have with respect to the stock market (Section 1):

1. Broker-related issues
    a. Brokerage
    b. App issues
    c. Security/Funds issues
    d. Any other
2. Research analyst or investment advisor
3. Concern with a listed company
4. Algo software for trading
5. Profit-sharing scam
6. Ponzi scheme
7. Guaranteed returns fraud
8. Binary trading scam
9. Forex trading scam
10. WhatsApp group trading app scam
11. Financial influencer fraud
12. Collective investment scheme
13. Portfolio management service

Now, before we start talking about what comes under SEBI and what does not, we need to understand one thing: SEBI is a regulatory body for the securities market and the following entities come under its regulation (Section 2):

- Stockbrokers
- Listed companies
- Mutual funds

- Registrar and transfer agents
- Depository participant
- Investment advisor
- Research analyst
- Exchange
- Depository
- Debenture
- NSE-approved algo software
- Merchant bankers
- KYC registration agency
- Clearing corporations
- Portfolio managers
- Venture capital funds
- Alternative investment funds
- Credit-rating agencies
- Real-estate investment trust
- Infrastructure investment trust
- Vault managers

Thus, complaints and issues/concerns related to these entities primarily come under the professional interest of the regulator. Simply speaking, if you go ahead and file a complaint on the SEBI portal, SCORES or Smart ODR, you will be able to file complaints only against the entities listed above.

Here are the scams/frauds/entities that do not come under SEBI (Section 3):

- Unregistered collective schemes (Ponzi) such as Creditbulls, Infinite Beacon
- Binary trading software such as OlympTrade, Expert Option, Binomo
- Forex trading software such as Exness Trade, EvaTrade
- Cryptocurrency apps such as WazirX, CoinSwitch

- Unregistered algo software
- Profit-sharing frauds
- Social media financial influencers (though discussions are underway currently on this topic)
- Social media frauds via WhatsApp groups
- Anything and everything that is not listed in Section 2

What really happens when a financial influencer or an unregistered tip provider sells you something and you incur a loss? While you do have a case against the entity/person, keep your expectations low.

It is not SEBI's pain to directly handle such cases. However, since these cases are around tips by unregistered people who claim to be SEBI-registered or falsify their presence in general, SEBI 'may' take an interest. You won't be able to file a complaint at the SCORES portal but you can send an email to scores@sebi.gov.in.

Even if you get a template-based response, you need to respond. This is assuming you have written down every possible fraudulent activity and attached every proof (screenshot/recording/document). You need to understand that hundreds of such emails float in SEBI's email box every day and it becomes very easy for the regulator to filter out the ones without proper detailing. The ones that get looked at are the only ones they work on.

It also needs to be known that these cases take time to resolve. The best you will get back is the money you paid as a fee. In no way you are going to recover the losses you incurred based on the tips received. And we all know that the fee is pretty much a mediocre amount as compared to the actual loss one incurs in such cases.

In scams related to unregistered CIS, binary/forex trading, and WhatsApp group frauds, SEBI does absolutely nothing. The best NSE does is that once someone notifies them about such frauds happening locally or at a national level, they send an email with details of the fraudsters as an 'awareness advisory', and nothing else.

This has happened in multiple cases of Ponzi schemes, scammers doing profit sharing, guaranteed returns frauds and so on. Furthermore, there are a few other instances where you cannot call the SEBI. If you go to the new SCORES portal of SEBI and try to lodge a complaint, you will be shown this pop-up on the screen:

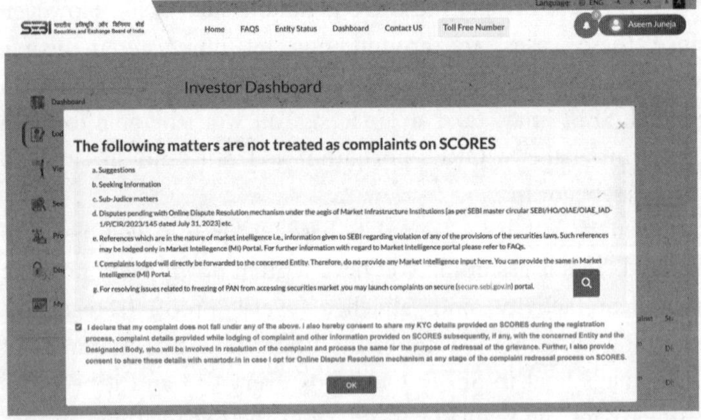

This tells you that SEBI won't treat the following as complaints and most likely won't take any action on them.

The list includes:

- If you are providing some sort of suggestion. There is a different mechanism for providing suggestions such as the consultation paper SEBI releases on various regulations.
- If you are seeking some sort of information from SEBI. It's better to file an RTI in that case.

- Any matters that are still in the court and are sub-judice in nature. SEBI won't get involved in any such matters.

Complaints that are being worked upon in Smart ODR, which is a separate portal and we have discussed it in another chapter. All complaints lodged there are taken care of by NSE and that is the only place to get such complaints resolved.

Any complaints regarding your frozen PAN card.

What's the Solution?

Honestly, there isn't one. If you want to avoid years of mental and financial stress, don't fall for such scams. It's good that you are reading this book which, hopefully, will help you in understanding the greys between the blacks and whites of the stock market.

Take heed of my advice about not falling for misinformation, lavish dreams and petty schemes. Good luck.

GLOSSARY

Advisory	A financial service where experts provide recommendations on investments, trading strategies, and portfolio management.
Algo trading (algorithmic trading)	The use of automated systems and algorithms to execute trades based on predefined criteria such as price, volume and timing without human intervention.
Algo-trading software	Automated trading systems that execute trades based on predefined algorithms and market conditions.
Alternative investment funds (AIFs)	Privately pooled investment funds that invest in assets beyond traditional stocks and bonds, such as hedge funds and private equity.
Back-testing	A simple way to check whether a trading strategy (that they are looking to use today) would have worked in the past or not. In back-testing, old market data is used to see how buying and selling decisions might have played out.
Bank Nifty	A stock index that tracks the performance of 12 major banking

	stocks on the National Stock Exchange (NSE).
Bank Nifty index number	The real-time value of the Bank Nifty index, reflecting the weighted performance of banking stocks within the index.
Binary trading	A high-risk financial instrument where traders bet on whether an asset's price will go up or down within a fixed time frame. Banned in India due to its speculative nature.
Block trade	A large-volume trade of securities executed outside the open market to minimize price fluctuations.
Bombay Stock Exchange (BSE)	It is Asia's oldest stock exchange, established in 1875, where stocks and securities are traded.
Brokerage	The fee or commission charged by brokers for executing trades on respective trading platforms.
Brokerage churning	Excessive trading by a broker in a client's account to generate commissions without regard for the client's best interest.
Clone trading apps	Fraudulent applications that mimic legitimate trading apps to scam investors by offering fake trades and siphoning money.
Credit-rating agencies	Organizations that assess the creditworthiness of entities issuing debt instruments such as bonds.
Dabba operators	Unauthorized entities running illegal

	trading setups outside recognized stock exchanges.
Dabba trading	An illegal trading practice operating parallel to the Indian stock market where orders are marked but not executed on any exchange. These are majorly run by dabba operators with transactions happening in cash.
Debentures	Long-term debt instruments issued by companies or governments to raise capital with a fixed interest rate.
Demat account	An electronic account used to hold shares and securities in digital format, required for trading in the stock market.
Depository participants (DPs)	Entities registered with depositories like NSDL and CDSL to facilitate the holding and transfer of securities in electronic form.
Derivatives trading	Trading of financial contracts whose value is derived from underlying assets such as stocks, commodities, or indices.
Discount broker	A brokerage firm offering trading services at lower costs but without additional advisory services.
Expiry day	The last trading day of a derivative contract (options or futures), after which the contract expires and is

	either settled or exercised.
Finfluencers	Financial influencers who provide investment and trading advice on social media platforms.
Forex trading (foreign exchange trading)	The trading of global currencies in the foreign exchange market, regulated in India with specific currency pairs allowed by SEBI and RBI.
Front-running	An illegal practice where an advisor, trader or broker places a trade on a specific security first and then passes on the same trade as a market recommendation to others.
Hedging	A risk management strategy used to offset potential losses in an investment by taking an opposite position in a related asset.
Index	A statistical measure representing the performance of a group of stocks in the market. Examples include Nifty 50, Sensex, and Bank Nifty.
Index-based derivatives trading	Trading in futures and options contracts based on stock market indices rather than individual stocks.
Infrastructure investment trust (InvIT)	A trust that pools investments to manage infrastructure projects and provides investors with dividends.
Initial public offering (IPO)	The process by which a private company offers its shares to the public for the first time to raise capital by listing on a stock exchange.
Intraday trading	Buying and selling stocks within the

	same trading session to capitalize on small price movements.
Investment advisors (IA)	SEBI-registered professionals or firms that provide financial advice and investment recommendations for a fee.
Midcap Nifty	A stock market index that represents the performance of 100 companies listed in NSE ranked between large-cap and small-cap categories.
Mutual fund	An investment vehicle that pools money from multiple investors to invest in diversified financial instruments.
National Stock Exchange (NSE)	India's leading stock exchange, known for its electronic trading platform and benchmark indices like Nifty 50.
Nifty 50	A stock market index representing India's 50 largest and most traded companies listed on the NSE.
NISM certification	A certification from the National Institute of Securities Markets (NISM) mandatory for professionals working in different segments of the stock market.
Options trading	A form of derivative trading where traders buy or sell contracts giving them the right (but not the obligation) to buy (call option) or sell (put option) an underlying asset at a predetermined price before a specific expiry date.

PE ratio (price-to-earnings ratio)	A financial metric used to evaluate a company's valuation by dividing its market price per share by earnings per share.
Ponzi scheme	A fraudulent investment scheme that pays returns to earlier investors using funds from new investors rather than actual profits.
Portfolio management services (PMS)	A service where professional portfolio managers manage investments on behalf of clients.
Real estate investment trust (REIT)	A company that owns, operates or finances income-generating real estate and allows investors to invest in properties.
Registered advisory	Investment advisory firms or individuals registered with SEBI or other regulatory bodies to provide financial and investment advice.
Research analyst (RA)	A SEBI-registered professional who conducts research and analysis on stocks, industries and financial markets to provide investment recommendations.
Retail traders	Individual investors who buy and sell securities for personal accounts rather than for an institution.
Scalping	A trading strategy that involves making multiple small trades throughout the day to capitalize on minor price fluctuations.
SEBI Complaints	An online platform where investors

Redress System (SCORES)	can Redress System (SCORES) file complaints against stockbrokers, investment advisors and other market participants.
Securities and Exchange Board of India (SEBI)	The regulatory body overseeing India's securities market to protect investors and ensure fair market practices.
Sensex	The benchmark index of the Bombay Stock Exchange (BSE), comprising 30 large, actively traded stocks representing various sectors.
Smart ODR (online dispute resolution)	A digital dispute resolution platform introduced by SEBI.
Stock exchange	A regulated marketplace where securities such as stocks and bonds are bought and sold.
Stock pathshala	An educational platform providing training, webinars and learning resources on stock market trading and investment strategies.
Stockbrokers	SEBI-registered intermediaries who facilitate buying and selling of stocks and other securities on behalf of clients.
Stop loss	A pre-set order to sell a security when it reaches a specific price to limit losses in trading.
Sub-broker	An agent working under a stockbroker to facilitate trading activities for clients.
Swing trading	A trading strategy where stocks

	are held for a few days or weeks to capitalize on short- to medium-term price movements.
Target price	The expected price level at which a trader or analyst anticipates a stock will reach based on analysis.
Trading account	A brokerage account that allows investors to buy and sell securities in financial markets.
Unauthorized trading	Trading activities conducted by brokers without the consent of their clients.
Unregistered advisory	Individuals or entities offering investment advice without proper registration.
Vault managers	Entities responsible for securely storing financial assets like gold and other commodities on behalf of investors.